ADVENTIST Potluck COOKBOOK

Favorite vegetarian recipes from fellowship halls across the country

DEBBY SHABO WADE

Pacific Press® Publishing Association
Nampa, Idaho
Oshawa, Ontario, Canada

Cover and inside illustration and design: Michelle C. Petz

Copyright © 1998 by
Pacific Press® Publishing Association
Printed in the United States
All Rights Reserved

Library of Congress Cataloging-in-Publication Data

Wade, Debby, 1951–
    Adventist potluck cookbook : favorite vegetarian recipes from fellowship halls
across the country / Debby Shabo Wade.
      p. cm. — (The adventist kitchen ; 1)
    ISBN 0-8163-1701-1 (pbk.)
    1. Vegetarian cookery.   I. Title.   II. Series.
TX837.W143 1999
641.5′636—dc21
                                            98-53229
                                              CIP

Contents

Dedication

To my fantastic family—
Ken, my husband of 26 years, and my sons, Adam and Seth,
who have been loyal fans of my experimentation in the kitchen through the years.
Without their support I would never have had the courage to tackle and complete this task.

Introduction

You know the drill . . . five o'clock Friday afternoon the phone rings. It's Patsy: "I'm fresh out of ideas. What are you bringing to potluck tomorrow?"

"Tomorrow's potluck Sabbath?" you exclaim. You've hardly thought about what's for supper tonight yet!

Most Adventist women have been there, done that. So, what do you do? Run to the pantry for Rice Krispies® and marshmallow cream to throw together an instant, unimaginative, horribly unhealthy dessert and hope someone else planned far enough ahead to supply the entrees? What if you had a book on your shelf that was full of tasty, innovative, quick, and easy-to-prepare dishes that were perfect for taking to an Adventist potluck?

If you did, it would be this book.

I took a home economics major in college (OK, I know it dates me), but since graduation most of my cooking has been for family, friends, and potlucks, with a few cooking schools thrown in for good measure. My husband, Ken, pastored four churches for quite a few years, so you can imagine how many potlucks I've been to! And whenever I tasted something I especially liked, I'd ask for the recipe. Many of those old recipes are still scrawled on the scraps of paper or 3 x 5 cards that happened to be at hand at the time. Through the years I've used, adapted, and shared many of these recipes with others.

In talking with the editorial group at Pacific Press®, we came up with the idea of soliciting recipes from other friends all over the world (we also worked at the General Conference for quite a few years, and spent four years in the Far East). I was positively overwhelmed by the response I got when I asked people for recipes. Thank you everyone for sharing! If you don't see one of your recipes in this book, I have heard rumors of a possible Book 2, so stay tuned! Thank you also to Deanna Davis for her expertise with the Potluck stories throughout the book.

Bringing all these recipes together in a book has been an exciting challenge, and lots of fun—especially as I tried out new recipes on my family.

NUTRITIONAL DATA

I know that these days a lot of people are watching what they eat more carefully—and potlucks have a notoriously bad image when it comes to healthful food. Many want to be careful of their sodium, fat, cholesterol, and sugar intake, so every recipe in this book gives a nutritional analysis. I didn't leave out recipes just because they were too high in fat, but for many you'll see an alternative light version listed on the same page. I created these alternative recipes when a given dish needed modification of several ingredients to bring the fat content down.

Other recipes that could be "defatted" by changing only one or two ingredients have suggested modifications, and the nutritional analysis column has two different sets of data, one for the regular recipe and the other for the light recipe.

One word of caution is in order when considering how to lower the amount of fat in a recipe. As I did the analysis of these recipes, I noticed that substituting low-fat or no-fat mayonnaise and some other reduced-fat products had the counterproductive effect of raising the amount of sodium in the recipe, so if sodium is an important consideration in your diet, watch the analysis figures carefully.

For those interested in some further creative ideas for cutting back on fat and cholesterol, I've included a section at the end, just before the index, with a few additional suggestions for ways to make things taste good on a low-fat, low-cholesterol diet. You can experiment further, if you wish.

WHAT YOU'LL FIND

You'll find ideas for drinks, salads, breads, entrees, vegetables, and desserts here. Most people don't bring appetizers, soups, or sandwiches to a potluck, so I haven't included any recipes for them.

The table of contents will guide you quickly to the section you want. If you're looking for a particular type of recipe, try the index at the end, which is divided by sections and type of dish. But if you're like me, what you really want to do is start reading through the recipes at random, looking for a new idea to wow the potluck line with next week. So . . . dive in! And happy potlucking!

Drinks

Bubbly Red Punch

Makes 20 servings

2 46-ounce cans Hawaiian Punch®, chilled
2 quarts ginger ale, chilled

In a one gallon container, mix Hawaiian Punch and ginger ale. Serve over ice.

VARIATIONS: Use any frozen, canned, or powdered fruit juice.

Blessed is he that expects nothing for he shall never be disappointed.

PER SERVING

Calories	95
Total Fat	0g
Sat. Fat	0g
Cholesterol	0g
Sodium	36mg
Total Carb.	24g
Dietary Fiber	0.1g
Protein	0g

Party Punch

RHONDA HAMES

Makes 25 servings

6 medium bananas
1 12-ounce can frozen pink lemonade concentrate
6 3/4 cups water
1 6-ounce can frozen orange juice concentrate

1/2 cup honey
2 quarts ginger ale, chilled
1 lime, sliced (for garnish)

Blend bananas and lemonade in blender for 15 seconds. Pour into a large bowl. Add water, orange juice, and honey; stir. Freeze in a covered container overnight or until slushy (about 2 hours).

Set out one hour before serving (to serve for potluck take out at 11:00 am—right before the sermon), in order to partially thaw. When ready to serve, add ginger ale and lime slices.

You are sure to get wonderful comments on this punch.

PER SERVING	
Calories	108
Total Fat	0.2g
Sat. Fat	0.1g
Cholesterol	0mg
Sodium	9mg
Total Carb.	28g
Dietary Fiber	0.8g
Protein	0.5g

Sparkling Cranberry Punch

Makes 20 servings

2 quarts cranberry juice cocktail, chilled
1 6-ounce frozen white lemonade concentrate
1 quart ginger ale, chilled

In a large container, combine cranberry cocktail and lemonade concentrate. Stir in ginger ale. Serve over ice.

PER SERVING

Calories	89
Total Fat	0.1g
Sat. Fat	0g
Cholesterol	0mg
Sodium	6mg
Total Carb.	23g
Dietary Fiber	0.1g
Protein	0g

Delicious Punch

Mary Barger

Makes 20 servings

2 12-ounce cans frozen white lemonade concentrate
32 ounces ginger ale, chilled
2 quarts frozen pineapple sherbet, softened
2 cups water

In a gallon container, empty frozen lemonade. Add ginger ale, softened pineapple sherbet, and water; stir. Serve over ice. If using a punch bowl, add ice after the punch is poured in.

This punch is almost white and is suitable for weddings, bridal showers, and anniversary celebrations as well as potlucks.

Little is much when God is in it.

PER SERVING

Calories	186
Total Fat	1g
Sat. Fat	1g
Cholesterol	4mg
Sodium	41mg
Total Carb.	44g
Dietary Fiber	0.5g
Protein	1g

Fruit Punch

Makes 22 servings

1 6-ounce can frozen orange juice concentrate
1 6-ounce can frozen white lemonade concentrate
1 12-ounce can frozen apple juice concentrate
2 quarts ginger ale, chilled
1 pint frozen orange sherbet

In a large container, combine concentrates. Pour in ginger ale. When ready to serve, spoon sherbet into container. Serve over ice.

PER SERVING

Calories	107
Total Fat	0.4g
Sat. Fat	0.2g
Cholesterol	1mg
Sodium	19mg
Total Carb.	26g
Dietary Fiber	0.2g
Protein	0.5g

Tropical Punch

Makes 30 servings

1 46-ounce can unsweetened pineapple juice, chilled
1 46-ounce can orange-grapefruit juice, chilled
2 quarts lemon-lime soda, chilled
1 pint frozen orange sherbet

In a large container, stir together juices and lemon-lime soda. Spoon sherbet into container when ready to serve. Serve over ice.

PER SERVING

Calories	87
Total Fat	0.3g
Sat. Fat	0.2g
Cholesterol	0.7mg
Sodium	15mg
Total Carb.	21g
Dietary Fiber	0.2g
Protein	0.5g

Lemonade

Makes 10 servings

6 1/2 cups cold water
1 cup lemon juice concentrate
1 cup granulated sugar

In a 2-quart pitcher, combine ingredients and stir until sugar dissolves. Serve over ice.

PER SERVING

Calories	83
Total Fat	0.1g
Sat. Fat	0g
Cholesterol	0mg
Sodium	10mg
Total Carb.	21g
Dietary Fiber	0.1g
Protein	0.1g

Russian Tea

ALTHEA BUCKINGHAM

Makes 35 servings

2 cups Tang® powder
1 10-ounce container Country Time® Lemonade Iced Tea Mix (decaffeinated)
1 1/2 teaspoons ground cinnamon
1 1/2 teaspoons ground nutmeg
1 teaspoon ground cloves

In a medium mixing bowl, combine all ingredients. Store in an air-tight container.

When ready to use, spoon 1 to 3 teaspoons into a mug of boiling water.

SERVING SUGGESTION: This drink is really nice at a potluck if you can have a percolator of hot water sitting on the counter and a canister of the Russian Tea beside it so people can help themselves and make the drink as strong as they want it. Great on a cold winter day. Can be iced as well in hot weather.

PER SERVING	
Calories	91
Total Fat	0.1g
Sat. Fat	0g
Cholesterol	0mg
Sodium	2mg
Total Carb.	23g
Dietary Fiber	0.1g
Protein	0.1g

SECTION 2

Breads

Angel Biscuits

Makes 22 biscuits

1/3 cup warm water (105° to 115° F)
1 package active dry yeast
1 tablespoon brown sugar
2 1/2 cups unbleached white flour
1 1/2 teaspoons baking powder

1/2 teaspoon baking soda
1/4 teaspoon salt
1/3 cup shortening
3/4 cup cultured buttermilk—from skim milk
  (or soured milk*)

In a small bowl, combine water, yeast, and brown sugar. Let stand until foamy.

In a large bowl, stir together flour, baking powder, baking soda, and salt. Using a pastry blender, cut in the shortening. Add the yeast mixture and buttermilk and stir until a soft dough forms. Knead on a lightly floured surface for 30 seconds. Pat or roll to 1/2" thick. Cut with a biscuit cutter, rerolling and cutting the scraps of dough. Place on ungreased baking sheet. Bake at 450° F for 7 to 9 minutes or until golden brown.

*IF YOU DON'T HAVE BUTTERMILK USE THIS:
In a 1-cup glass measuring cup, measure 1 tablespoon lemon juice or vinegar, then add enough 1% low-fat milk to measure 1 cup. Let stand for 5 minutes.

Some people who say "our Father" on Sabbath go around the rest of the week acting like orphans.

PER SERVING

Calories	84
Total Fat	3g
Sat. Fat	1g
Cholesterol	2mg
Sodium	278mg
Total Carb.	11g
Dietary Fiber	0.5g
Protein	2g

Herbed Cottage Cheese Scones

Makes 12 scones

2 cups unbleached white flour
3 tablespoons brown sugar
2 teaspoons baking powder
1/2 teaspoon baking soda
1/2 teaspoon ground dried mustard
1/2 teaspoon rosemary

1/4 teaspoon ground sage
Pinch of salt
3 tablespoons margarine
1 large egg white
1 cup cottage cheese (large or small curd)
1/3 cup skim milk

In a large bowl, combine flour, brown sugar, baking powder, baking soda, mustard, rosemary, sage, and salt. Using a pastry blender cut in the margarine. Set aside.

In a small bowl, combine the egg white, cottage cheese, and milk. Add all at once to the flour mixture and stir just until a soft dough forms. Knead on a lightly floured surface for 30 seconds. Pat into an greased 8" cake pan. Brush dough with a little additional milk. Bake at 425° F for 22 to 25 minutes or until golden brown.

PER SERVING

Calories	122
Total Fat	3g
Sat. Fat	0.6g
Cholesterol	1mg
Sodium	411mg
Total Carb.	18g
Dietary Fiber	0.6g
Protein	5g

Potato-Chive Rolls

Makes 24 rolls

4 1/2 to 5 cups unbleached white flour
1 cup instant potato flakes
1 tablespoon granulated sugar
4 teaspoons dried chives
2 teaspoons salt

2 packages active dry yeast
2 cups skim milk
1/2 cup sour cream (fat-free can be used)
2 eggs (or 1/2 cup egg substitute)

In a large bowl, combine 1 1/2 cups flour, potato flakes, sugar, chives, salt, and yeast; mix well.

In a small saucepan, heat milk and sour cream until very warm (120° to 130° F).

Add warm liquid to flour mixture. Beat in eggs. Beat 2 to 3 minutes. Stir in additional flour to form a stiff dough. Place dough in large, greased bowl. Cover and let rise till doubled (about 45 to 55 minutes).

Grease a 9" x 13" baking pan. On well-floured surface, knead enough flour into dough till it is no longer sticky. Divide dough into 24 pieces and shape into balls. Place in baking pan. Cover and let rise until doubled (about 30 to 35 minutes). Bake at 375° F for 25 to 35 minutes or until golden brown. Remove from pan and cool on wire racks.

PER SERVING

Calories	115
Total Fat	1g
Sat. Fat	1g
Cholesterol	18mg
Sodium	509mg
Total Carb.	21g
Dietary Fiber	1g
Protein	4g

Harvest Muffins

Makes 20 muffins

1 cup granulated sugar*
2 cups unbleached white flour
2 teaspoons ground cinnamon
2 teaspoons baking soda
1/2 teaspoon salt
1/2 cups chopped pecans
1/2 cup grated coconut (optional)

1/2 cup raisins
2 cups grated carrots
1 medium apple, grated
3 eggs*
1 cup canola oil*
1 1/2 teaspoons vanilla extract

In a large bowl, combine dry ingredients. Set aside.

In a medium bowl, combine raisins, carrots, apples, eggs, oil, and vanilla.

Pour liquid mixture all at once into dry ingredients. Mix gently just until moistened. Fill greased muffin cups 2/3 full. Bake at 350° F for 15 to 18 minutes or until golden. Turn onto cookie racks to cool.

*LITE VERSION SUBSTITUTION

2/3 cup granulated sugar
3/4 cup egg substitute
1/2 cup Prune Whip (see p. 155)

PER SERVING

Calories	242
Total Fat	14g
Sat. Fat	2g
Cholesterol	28mg
Sodium	362mg
Total Carb.	26g
Dietary Fiber	2g
Protein	2g

LITE SERVING

Calories	119
Total Fat	1g
Sat. Fat	0.2g
Cholesterol	0.2mg
Sodium	365mg
Total Carb.	25g
Dietary Fiber	1g
Protein	2g

Pineapple-Date Bran Muffins

Makes 12 muffins

1 1/4 cups unbleached white flour
2 tablespoons granulated sugar
1 tablespoon baking powder
1/4 teaspoon salt
2 cups All-Bran® cereal

1 1/4 cups skim milk
1/2 of a 20-ounce can crushed pineapple, drained
1/2 cup pitted dates
1/4 cup egg substitute
2 tablespoons Prune Whip (see p. 155)

In a medium bowl, stir flour, sugar, baking powder, and salt. Set aside.

In a large bowl, combine All-Bran, milk, drained pineapple, and dates. Let stand about 5 minutes. Add egg substitute and Prune Whip and mix well. Add flour mixture, stirring only until combined. Fill greased cups of a muffin tin 2/3 full. Bake at 350° F for 18 to 20 minutes or until lightly browned.

The wages of sin is death, but by receiving Christ you can leave before payday.

PER SERVING

Calories	92
Total Fat	0.5g
Sat. Fat	0.1g
Cholesterol	0.5mg
Sodium	358mg
Total Carb.	20g
Dietary Fiber	1g
Protein	3g

Company Cornbread

Makes 15 servings

1/3 cup diced green chilies
2/3 cup granulated sugar
1/2 cup margarine
4 eggs (or 1 cup egg substitute)
1 16-ounce can cream-style corn
1/2 cup grated Monterey Jack cheese

1/2 cup grated cheddar cheese
1 cup unbleached white flour
1 cup yellow cornmeal
4 teaspoons baking powder
1/4 teaspoon salt

Combine all ingredients in a large bowl. Stir until mixed. Pour into a greased 9" x 13" baking dish. Bake 350° F for 25 to 30 minutes or until toothpick inserted into the center of the bread comes out clean.

PER SERVING

Calories	234
Total Fat	11g
Sat. Fat	4g
Cholesterol	62mg
Sodium	484mg
Total Carb.	27g
Dietary Fiber	1g
Protein	6g

Italian Bread Ring

Makes 24 servings

2 tablespoons sesame seeds
4 1/2 to 5 1/4 cups unbleached white flour
1/4 cup granulated sugar
1 1/2 teaspoons salt
2 packages active dry yeast
1 cup water
1 cup skim milk

1/3 cup margarine
2 eggs (optional)

Filling:
1 cup grated mozzarella cheese
1/2 teaspoon Italian seasoning
1/4 teaspoon garlic powder
1/4 cup margarine

Generously grease a 10" Bundt pan and sprinkle with sesame seeds.

In a large bowl, combine 2 1/2 cups flour, sugar, salt, and yeast. Set aside.

In a small saucepan, heat water, milk, and 1/3 cup margarine until very warm (120° to 130° F). Remove from heat and add to flour mixture. Stir. Add eggs. Beat dough for 2 to 3 minutes. Stir in enough flour to form a stiff batter.

In a small bowl, combine mozzarella cheese, seasonings, and 1/4 cup margarine. Mix well.

Spoon half of batter into prepared Bundt pan. With fingers spread cheese filling evenly over batter to within 1/2" of sides of pan. Spoon remaining batter over filling. Cover and let rise till doubled (about 30 minutes). Bake at 350° F for 30 to 40 minutes or until golden brown. Turn out onto cooling rack.

PER SERVING	
Calories	167
Total Fat	6g
Sat. Fat	1g
Cholesterol	18mg
Sodium	511mg
Total Carb.	22g
Dietary Fiber	1g
Protein	5g

Raisin & Cracked Wheat Bread

Makes 80 half-slice servings

1 1/2 cups cracked wheat (bulgur)

1 cup raisins

1/2 cup brown sugar

2 teaspoons salt

3 tablespoons margarine

2 cups boiling water

2 packages active dry yeast

2/3 cup warm water (105° to 115° F)

5 to 6 cups unbleached white flour

1 egg, beaten

In a large bowl, combine cracked wheat, raisins, brown sugar, salt, margarine, and 2 cups boiling water. Mix well and cool to 105° to 115° F.

After the cracked wheat has cooled, dissolve yeast in 2/3 cups warm water in a small bowl. Add to cooled cracked wheat mixture. Add 2 cups flour and beat for several minutes. By hand, stir in enough flour till hard to handle, then turn out onto a floured surface, kneading in more flour till dough is smooth. Place dough in large, clean, lightly greased bowl. Cover and let rise until doubled (45 to 60 minutes). Punch down and divide dough in half. Shape into balls and place on greased cookie sheet. Cover and let rise until doubled. Heat oven to 350° F.

With a sharp knife, slash a 1/2" deep lattice design on top of each loaf. Brush with beaten egg and bake for 35 to 45 minutes or until loaves sound hollow when tapped. Cool on wire racks after removing from cookie sheet.

Take my word for it, when the church members see this bread at potluck, there will be a grabbing frenzy to be sure to get a piece. Since the loaves are so large, slice each loaf into 20 pieces; then cut each piece in half. This will ensure enough to go around at potluck.

PER SERVING

Calories	50
Total Fat	0.6g
Sat. Fat	0.1g
Cholesterol	2mg
Sodium	159mg
Total Carb.	10g
Dietary Fiber	1g
Protein	1g

Chicago Pizza Crust

Makes 15 servings

1 1/4 cups warm water (105° to 115° F)
1 tablespoon active dry yeast
1 tablespoon granulated sugar
1/4 cup canola oil
2 1/2 to 3 cups unbleached white flour
1 teaspoon salt

In a large bowl, combine warm water, yeast, and sugar. Set aside and let foam. When foam has formed, add oil, salt, and 1 1/2 cups flour. Stir until mixed, then beat for 1 minute. Add enough flour to make a firm dough, then turn dough out onto counter and knead, incorporating enough flour so dough is not sticky.

Place dough in a clean, greased bowl. Cover and let rise for 15 minutes. Spread with fingers in greased pizza pan that has been sprinkled with yellow corn meal.

SERVING SUGGESTION: You can use this for the Garden Pizza (see p. 96) base or create your own pizza. For pizza, just add your favorite spaghetti sauce and favorite toppings. Top with cheese and bake at 350° F for 15 to 20 minutes or until golden.

PER SERVING

Calories	126
Total Fat	4g
Sat. Fat	0.4g
Cholesterol	0mg
Sodium	473mg
Total Carb.	19g
Dietary Fiber	0.8g
Protein	3g

✪Oatmeal-Wheat Germ Crackers

SETH WADE

Makes 60 crackers

3 cups quick oatmeal
2 cups unbleached white flour
1 cup wheat germ (raw or toasted)
3 tablespoons granulated sugar

1 teaspoon salt
3/4 cup canola oil
1 cup water
Sesame or poppy seeds (optional)

In a large bowl, combine quick oats, flour, wheat germ, sugar, and salt. Set aside.

In a small bowl, combine oil and water. Stir briskly; add all at once to dry mixture. Stir until dough forms a ball. Divide dough into 4 balls. While working with first ball, keep other dough covered.

On an ungreased cookie sheet, roll ball of dough until cracker-thin. Sprinkle lightly with salt and, if you desire, sesame or poppy seeds. Press in seeds with the rolling pin. Score the rolled dough with a pizza cutter to desired cracker sizes (nutritional information is based on 1/60 of the recipe). Bake at 350° F for 12 to 15 minutes or until golden brown. *The outside crackers may brown faster than the inside crackers, so you may want to cool the outside crackers on a wire rack and re-insert the cookie sheet into the oven to finish baking the remaining crackers.* Cool on a wire rack.

This is always a hit. Please see Section 7 of the cookbook for spreads and ideas on how to serve crackers.

PER SERVING

Calories	78
Total Fat	3g
Sat. Fat	0.4g
Cholesterol	0mg
Sodium	92mg
Total Carb.	10g
Dietary Fiber	1g
Protein	2g

Salads

Creamy Frozen Fruit Salad

Makes 10 servings

1 16-ounce can fruit cocktail
1 8 3/4-ounce can crushed pineapple
1 16-ounce can pitted sweet cherries
1 8-ounce package cream cheese, softened

1 cup sour cream
1/4 cup granulated sugar
1 cup miniature marshmallows

In strainer, drain fruit cocktail, pineapple, and cherries.

In a large bowl, beat cream cheese, sour cream, and sugar until creamy. Stir drained fruits and marshmallows into cheese mixture. Pour into a large mold or loaf pan. Freeze overnight (or at least 8 hours).

Ten to 15 minutes before serving, remove mold from freezer and let stand at room temperature. Slice into serving sizes and arrange on a tray lined with leaf lettuce.

Tasty and beautiful.

PER SERVING

Calories	198
Total Fat	12g
Sat. Fat	8g
Cholesterol	35mg
Sodium	83mg
Total Carb.	19g
Dietary Fiber	1g
Protein	3g

Creative Fruit Salad

SUBMITTED BY DALE GALUSHA

It would be a typical church potluck, or so I thought. But one dear little old lady made it my most memorable. As I stood at the door greeting members, she walked in proudly carrying her potluck dish. "The Lord is good!" she announced suddenly. "Yes He is," I replied, "but why do you say so?" "He is good; I haven't been feeling very well, but I needed to make something for this potluck. The Lord impressed me to make a fruit salad. I thought I was mistaken; I wasn't feeling well, and I knew all the work it would take to prepare the fruit for this fruit salad. Then God impressed me to use my blender."

She triumphantly removed the lid to show me her puréed fruit salad. Having been blended the day before, it appeared to be previously digested and had turned a noxious brown.

The unique offering was put on the potluck table. Well, as you could expect, it was passed by—no one touched it—I was keeping track. I meant to do my duty and spoon some of the stuff onto my plate but got sidetracked in the kitchen. By the time I came out to do so, the little lady was snapping the lid back on her bowl. With a great-big smile she said to me, "God is good. I have a potluck to go to tomorrow, and now I won't have to fix anything new."

Curried Pasta and Fruit Salad

FriChik®

Makes 10 servings

1 1/3 cups uncooked pasta shells
1 tablespoon canola or olive oil

Dressing:
1 tablespoon olive oil
1/3 cup chopped white onion
2 teaspoons curry powder
1/2 cup plain yogurt
1/2 cup low-fat mayonnaise
3 tablespoons pickle relish
3/4 teaspoon salt

1 12.5-ounce can Worthington FriChik®, diced
1 1/2 cups seedless green grapes
1 1/2 cups cubed cantaloupe
3/4 cup sliced celery

Cook pasta according to package directions using 1 tablespoon of oil. Drain, rinse, and set aside.

In a small skillet, heat 1 tablespoon olive oil. Add onion and saute until tender. Add curry powder and cook to release flavors. Remove from heat and set aside.

In blender, combine yogurt, mayonnaise, pickle relish, salt, and onion mixture. Blend until smooth. Set aside.

In a large bowl, combine pasta, diced FriChik, grapes, cantaloupe, celery, and dressing. Toss well. Cover and chill in refrigerator overnight.

PER SERVING

Calories	106
Total Fat	7g
Sat. Fat	1g
Cholesterol	5mg
Sodium	311mg
Total Carb.	10g
Dietary Fiber	0.8g
Protein	1g

Frog-Eye Salad

JEAN CONEFF

Makes 25 servings

2/3 cup granulated sugar
2 tablespoons flour
1/2 teaspoon salt
1 3/4 cups pineapple juice
  (juice from canned pineapple + water)
2 eggs, beaten
3 quarts water
2 teaspoons salt

1 tablespoon canola oil
1 16-ounce package Acini de Pepe*
3 11-ounce cans mandarin oranges, drained
2 20-ounce cans pineapple chunks, drained (reserve juice)
1 20-ounce can crushed pineapple, drained (reserve juice)
1 16-ounce container Cool Whip® (approx.), thawed
1 cup miniature marshmallows (optional)
1 cup grated coconut (optional)

In a medium saucepan, combine sugar, flour, and salt. Gradually stir in pineapple juice and egg. Cook over moderate heat, stirring until thickened. Cool to room temperature. Set aside.

In a large kettle over medium-high heat, bring water, salt, and oil to a boil. Add Acini de Pepe. Cook at rolling boil until pasta is tender. Drain and rinse. Cool to room temperature.

In a large bowl, combine dressing and pasta. Mix lightly but thoroughly. Refrigerate overnight in an airtight container.

Remove pasta mixture from refrigerator. Add thoroughly-drained canned fruit and remaining ingredients to pasta mixture. Mix lightly but thoroughly. Refrigerate in an airtight container. *Salad may be refrigerated for as long as a week, so it is a really good make-ahead for potlucks.*

*A pasta product about the size of BBs. Generally sold in a box at the grocery store in the same section as other dry pastas.)

PER SERVING

Calories	183
Total Fat	5g
Sat. Fat	4g
Cholesterol	28mg
Sodium	254mg
Total Carb.	32g
Dietary Fiber	2g
Protein	3g

☆Orange-Buttermilk Jell-O☆

SHIRLEY JUHL

Makes 8 servings

2 cups reconstituted frozen orange juice
1 3-ounce package orange Jell-O®
2 cups buttermilk

In a small saucepan bring orange juice to a boil. Dissolve the orange Jell-O in orange juice. Remove from heat and add buttermilk. Pour into a mold. Refrigerate until ready to serve.

Unmold onto platter and garnish with red leaf lettuce and fresh fruit of your choice.

You would think it was orange sherbet. Sooo easy. Try adding fruits or vegetables to the Jell-O for variations.

PER SERVING

Calories	93
Total Fat	1g
Sat. Fat	0.4g
Cholesterol	2mg
Sodium	92mg
Total Carb.	19g
Dietary Fiber	0.1g
Protein	3g

Four-Bean Salad

Makes 15 servings

1 14 1/2-ounce can cut green beans
1 14 1/2-ounce can cut yellow beans
1 14 1/2-ounce can red kidney beans
1 14 1/2-ounce can garbanzo beans
1/2 cup canola oil

1/2 cup white vinegar (or lemon juice)
3/4 cup granulated sugar
1 teaspoon salt
1/2 cup chopped green pepper
1 medium white onion, sliced

Using strainer, drain all beans.

In a medium bowl, mix oil, vinegar, sugar, and salt. Set aside.

In a large bowl, combine beans, green pepper, and onion. Pour dressing over beans. Stir gently. Set in refrigerator until potluck.

A good make-ahead recipe.

PER SERVING	
Calories	164
Total Fat	7g
Sat. Fat	0.7g
Cholesterol	0mg
Sodium	437mg
Total Carb.	22g
Dietary Fiber	3g
Protein	3g

Green Bean Salad With Walnuts and Feta Cheese

Makes 10 servings

1 1/2 pounds green beans, ends trimmed, cut in half
3/4 cup olive oil
1/2 cup finely-chopped mint (or parsley), packed
1/4 cup white wine vinegar
3/4 teaspoon salt

1 clove garlic, minced
1 cup toasted coarsely-chopped walnuts
1 cup diced red onion
1 cup crumbled feta cheese

In a 6-quart kettle over medium-high heat, bring water to a boil. Add fresh green beans and cook until tender but crisp. Drain beans in a strainer and blanch in ice-cold water. (This stops the cooking process.) Drain. Store in container in refrigerator until ready to serve for potluck.

For dressing: Combine oil, mint, vinegar, salt, and garlic in blender. Mint should be well liquefied. Store in refrigerator until ready to serve salad.

Just before serving at potluck, place beans in a serving bowl. Sprinkle walnuts, onions, and feta cheese over top. Pour dressing over bean mixture and toss gently.

The combination of flavors is wonderful.

PER SERVING

Calories	289
Total Fat	26g
Sat. Fat	5g
Cholesterol	13mg
Sodium	348mg
Total Carb.	9g
Dietary Fiber	3g
Protein	7g

Lima Bean Salad

LYNDELLE CHIOMENTI

Makes 8 servings

2 10-ounce packages frozen Lima beans
1 medium bunch celery, sliced
2 16-ounce cans sliced black olives, drained
1 large bottle Italian salad dressing
  (Reduced-calorie dressing works very well.)

Garlic powder (to taste)
Ground oregano (to taste)
1 large white onion, sliced

Cook Lima beans according to package directions. Drain. While still warm, mix Lima beans with celery, olives, and salad dressing. Season to taste with garlic powder and oregano. Garnish salad with sliced onions. Marinate overnight in refrigerator until ready to serve.

PER SERVING	
Calories	166
Total Fat	6g
Sat. Fat	1g
Cholesterol	1mg
Sodium	528mg
Total Carb.	23g
Dietary Fiber	6g
Protein	6g

Artichoke Pasta Salad

Makes 8 servings

8 ounces uncooked linguine
1 14-ounce can water-packed artichoke hearts, drained
2/3 cup sliced black olives
1/4 cup olive oil

3 tablespoons lemon juice concentrate
2 cloves garlic, minced
3 dashes hot sauce
1/2 teaspoon salt

Cook linguine according to package directions. Drain, rinse, and set aside.

In a large bowl, quarter artichoke hearts. Add all remaining ingredients—except linguine. Let marinate for one hour. After an hour toss linguine with artichoke mixture. Refrigerate until ready to serve.

PER SERVING

Calories	188
Total Fat	9g
Sat. Fat	1g
Cholesterol	21mg
Sodium	404mg
Total Carb.	23g
Dietary Fiber	4g
Protein	5g

Lemon Lentil Pasta Salad

Makes 8 servings

1/2 cup lemon juice (fresh-squeezed or bottled)
1 1/2 teaspoons salt
1/4 cup olive oil
2 dashes hot sauce
2 cloves garlic, minced
2 cups uncooked lentils

4 cups water
2 cups uncooked pasta shells
2 stalks celery, thinly sliced
2/3 cup grated carrots
1/2 cup chopped fresh parsley (or mint)
1/2 cup pinenuts

In a small bowl, combine lemon juice, salt, olive oil, hot sauce, and garlic. Use wire whisk to blend. Refrigerate.

In a medium saucepan, combine lentils and 4 cups of water. Bring to a boil and reduce heat. Cover and simmer until lentils are tender but not mushy (about 15 minutes). Drain and rinse with cool water. Set aside.

Cook pasta according to package directions until shells are tender but still firm. Drain and rinse with cold water.

In a large bowl, combine pasta, lentils, and remainder of ingredients. Pour dressing over salad and toss gently. Refrigerate overnight.

SERVING SUGGESTION: Place leaf lettuce on a platter and spoon salad onto lettuce. Pretty.

PER SERVING	
Calories	158
Total Fat	4g
Sat. Fat	0.5g
Cholesterol	10mg
Sodium	236mg
Total Carb.	23g
Dietary Fiber	8g
Protein	8g

Vegetable Pasta Salad

Makes 6 servings

2 cups uncooked orzo*
2 cups water
2 cups crumbled feta cheese
1/2 cup chopped red onion
1 cup chopped green pepper

1/2 cup chopped red pepper
1/4 cup finely-chopped fresh parsley
1/4 cup sliced black olives
1/4 cup lemon juice
1 tablespoon olive oil

Cook orzo according to package directions. Don't use oil or salt. Drain and rinse with cold water. Set aside.

In a medium bowl, combine feta cheese, chopped vegetables, olives and orzo.

In a small bowl, combine lemon juice and olive oil. Pour over pasta mixture and toss gently. Refrigerate until ready to serve.

Very colorful.

PER SERVING

Calories	141
Total Fat	3g
Sat. Fat	1g
Cholesterol	32mg
Sodium	108mg
Total Carb.	24g
Dietary Fiber	1g
Protein	6g

*A small oval-shaped pasta. This can be found on the shelf with other dried pastas in your grocer's store.

Coleslaw Humor

SUBMITTED BY BEV BINDER

My sister, Judy, and her husband, Danny, have church potlucks at their house once in a while. Danny especially likes Judy's coleslaw. She fixes it more savory than sweet, and that's what he likes about it and looks forward to taking large helpings of it.

Well, as Danny was going through line this one Sabbath, he spotted what he thought was Judy's coleslaw and took a huge helping. Rather hungry and still in line, he decided to take a big mouthful of the coleslaw. This salad was sweet, complete with bananas. Being his vocal self, he blurted out, "Judy, what did you do to this salad?" There were a few moments of silence, and then the truth came out that the salad was not his wife's but another woman's. Suffice it to say that he all but crawled under the table.

Garden Patch Potato Salad

Makes 12 servings

8 cups cooked, peeled, and cubed potatoes
2 cups chopped fresh zucchini
1 cup thinly sliced celery
3/4 cup grated carrots
3 tablespoons finely-chopped onion
2 cups sour cream (lite sour cream can be substituted)

2 tablespoons vinegar or lemon juice
1 tablespoon granulated sugar
1 teaspoon salt
1/2 teaspoon dill weed
1/4 teaspoon celery salt

In a large bowl, combine cubed potatoes, zucchini, celery, carrots, and onion. Toss together lightly. Set aside.

In a small bowl, combine remaining ingredients. Mix well. Add to vegetables and mix lightly. Chill in refrigerator until ready to serve.

SERVING SUGGESTION: If you want to make this special, you can pour the salad into a lightly greased 3-quart bowl, or mold, and chill. When ready to serve, invert onto a bed of leaf lettuce and garnish. Beautiful.

PER SERVING

Calories	174
Total Fat	8g
Sat. Fat	5g
Cholesterol	17mg
Sodium	235mg
Total Carb.	23g
Dietary Fiber	2g
Protein	4g

Layered Green Salad

BUD ELMER

Makes 15 servings

1 medium head iceberg lettuce,
  torn into bite-sized pieces
1/2 to 1 cup sliced celery
1/2 cup chopped red, green, or yellow pepper
1/2 cup finely-chopped green onions

1 8-ounce can sliced water chestnuts
1 cup grated low-fat mozzarella cheese
1 10-ounce package frozen green peas, thawed
2 cups low-fat mayonnaise
2 tablespoons sugar

In a large see-through glass bowl, layer items as listed. *This is not a tossed salad.*

Cover with mayonnaise, leaving no cracks. Sprinkle sugar over mayonnaise. Cover tightly and refrigerate overnight. Just before serving, dig into the mayonnaise a little bit.

PER SERVING

Calories	177
Total Fat	12g
Sat. Fat	1g
Cholesterol	6mg
Sodium	338mg
Total Carb.	19g
Dietary Fiber	2g
Protein	5g

Madras Salad

Makes 12 servings

4 cups cooked white or brown rice
2 10-ounce packages frozen green peas, thawed
4 medium tomatoes, chopped
1/2 cup olive oil
1/2 cup minced onions

1/2 cup minced fresh parsley
6 tablespoons white vinegar or lemon juice
2 tablespoons chopped fresh basil
1/2 teaspoon salt

Cook rice according to package directions.

In a medium bowl, combine all ingredients with rice. Refrigerate until ready to serve.

PER SERVING

Calories	199
Total Fat	9g
Sat. Fat	1g
Cholesterol	0mg
Sodium	345mg
Total Carb.	25g
Dietary Fiber	3g
Protein	4g

Mediterranean Cashew Salad

PAT HABADA

Makes 8 servings

1 10-ounce package frozen green peas, thawed
1 cup sliced celery
1 cup chopped cauliflower
1/4 cup diced green onion

1 cup cashews (whole or pieces)*
1/2 cup sour cream (lite sour cream may be substituted)
1 cup fat-free ranch dressing
Salt to taste

This salad can be layered in a serving bowl and refrigerated overnight. When ready to serve simply mix the sour cream and ranch dressing together and toss with salad.

*Pine nuts can be used in place of the cashews.

PER SERVING	
Calories	215
Total Fat	11g
Sat. Fat	3g
Cholesterol	6mg
Sodium	412mg
Total Carb.	22g
Dietary Fiber	4g
Protein	5g

Entrees

Potluck Story

SUBMITTED BY PAT GILBERT

Mountain worship services were an annual event each summer at our church. Along with special programs, music and nature walks, was the midday potluck. We all had a big laugh on one of those mountain-worship Sabbaths when we lined up at the potluck table. There were a few desserts, two or three other dishes, AND baked beans AND baked beans AND baked beans AND more baked beans—at least 95 percent of the dishes brought were baked beans.

Everyone laughed and ate plenty of beans. We were thankful to be in the mountain air, which helped to dissipate the aftereffects!

P.S. Beano®, a food enzyme dietary supplement designed to prevent flatulence, is available at grocery stores, pharmacies, and any nutrition store.

Best Meatballs

CELESTE PERRINO WALKER

Makes 6 servings

1 cup crushed cheese crackers
1/2 cup ground pecans (or walnuts)
Garlic powder to taste
1 small onion, chopped

3 eggs*
1/2 cup grated cheddar cheese*
1/4 cup grated Parmesan cheese*

In a medium bowl, mix all ingredients. Form into balls and fry in small amount of oil in skillet.

*LITE VERSION SUBSTITUTION:

3/4 cup egg substitute
1/2 cup grated low-fat cheddar cheese
1/4 cup grated low-fat Swiss

SERVING SUGGESTION: Serve with your favorite sauce. Spaghetti sauce is nice.

PER SERVING

Calories	213
Total Fat	15g
Sat. Fat	5g
Cholesterol	120mg
Sodium	271mg
Total Carb.	9g
Dietary Fiber	1g
Protein	11g

LITE SERVING

Calories	205
Total Fat	13g
Sat. Fat	4g
Cholesterol	15mg
Sodium	251mg
Total Carb.	9g
Dietary Fiber	1g
Protein	12g

Cottage Cheese Balls

SUE SHABO

Makes 8 servings

1 cup cottage cheese (large or small curd)*	2 eggs*
1 cup quick oats	1 teaspoon ground sage
1 cup bread crumbs	1 teaspoon salt
1 medium onion, minced	Pinch of sugar

In a medium bowl, combine all ingredients, mixing well. Form into balls and fry in a small amount of oil in a skillet over medium-high heat. (Or if you prefer, place balls on a lightly greased cookie sheet and bake in the oven at 375° F for 20 to 25 minutes.) Place cooked meatballs in a 9" x 13" baking dish. Cover with one can low-fat mushroom soup mixed with 1 can of water. Bake at 350° F for 30 minutes.

* LITE VERSION SUBSTITUTION
1 cup 1% lowfat cottage cheese (large or small curd)
1/2 cup egg substitute

PER SERVING

Calories	182
Total Fat	4g
Sat. Fat	1g
Cholesterol	57mg
Sodium	537mg
Total Carb.	25g
Dietary Fiber	3g
Protein	10g

LITE SERVING

Calories	168
Total Fat	3g
Sat. Fat	0.7g
Cholesterol	1mg
Sodium	550mg
Total Carb.	25g
Dietary Fiber	3g
Protein	10g

Debby's Meatless Meatballs

Makes 12 servings

1 cup finely-chopped walnuts
1 cup cracker crumbs
1 cup finely-chopped onion
1/2 cup grated cheddar cheese

1 tablespoon dried parsley
1/2 teaspoon salt
1/2 teaspoon ground sage
5 large eggs*

If you don't want to do all the chopping by hand, use your food processor, even your blender. The walnuts and crackers blend very well. To blend onions, put about 2 cups of water in your blender and quickly pulse to chop the onion. Drain.

In a medium bowl, combine all ingredients after they have been chopped, etc. Stir and form into balls.

In a skillet over medium-high heat, fry meatballs in a small amount of oil until golden brown.

*Lite Version Substitution
1 1/4 cups egg substitute

Serving Suggestion: These can be placed in a baking dish in the oven with your favorite sauce. I like to put them in a large skillet on the stove over medium-high heat with the following sauce:

In a small bowl, mix 1 can tomato soup and 1 1/2 cans water. Beat until smooth. Add to the meatballs and simmer for 20 minutes over medium-high heat uncovered. *The sauce will boil down and become thicker.*

PER SERVING	
Calories	177
Total Fat	11g
Sat. Fat	3g
Cholesterol	99mg
Sodium	189mg
Total Carb.	10g
Dietary Fiber	1g
Protein	9g

LITE SERVING	
Calories	168
Total Fat	10g
Sat. Fat	2g
Cholesterol	11mg
Sodium	210mg
Total Carb.	10g
Dietary Fiber	1g
Protein	9g

Low-fat Meatballs

NATHALIE BISCHOFF (ADAPTED BY AUTHOR)

Makes 12 servings

1 cup egg substitute
1 20-ounce can Worthington Low Fat
   Vegetarian Burger™, crumbled*
1 medium onion, chopped
3 cloves garlic, minced
2/3 cup finely-chopped walnuts
1 cup seasoned bread crumbs
2/3 cup grated low-fat mozzarella cheese
1/2 teaspoon garlic powder
1 teaspoon McKay's® Chicken-style Seasoning
1 teaspoon poultry seasoning

Sauce:
1/2 cup finely-chopped onion
1 1/2 cups tomato sauce
2 tablespoons lemon juice
2 tablespoons molasses
1 clove garlic, minced
1/3 cup honey
1 tablespoon soy sauce
1/2 teaspoon garlic powder
2 teaspoons onion powder
2 teaspoons dried parsley

In a large bowl, combine ingredients—except those for the sauce—and mix well. Shape into 24 balls and place in a greased 9" x 13" baking dish. Bake at 350° F for 30 to 40 minutes.

In a medium bowl, combine sauce ingredients. Remove meatballs from oven and pour sauce over them. Return dish to oven and bake 25 minutes longer. Reheat for potluck.

The fact that you don't fry these meatballs in oil is a winner, and it doesn't affect the flavor!

*For a great variation, substitute 1 16-ounce roll of frozen Morningstar Farms Ground Meatless® for the canned burger. Both can be purchased at your local ABC. The flavor is outstanding!

PER SERVING	
Calories	156
Total Fat	6g
Sat. Fat	1g
Cholesterol	1mg
Sodium	612mg
Total Carb.	11g
Dietary Fiber	2g
Protein	14g

Tofu Cheese Balls

Makes 8 servings

1 cup crumbled soft tofu
1 cup quick oatmeal
1 cup bread crumbs
1 medium onion, minced

1/2 cup egg substitute
1 teaspoon ground sage
1 teaspoon salt
Pinch of sugar

garlic
chopped nuts, (opt.)

In a medium bowl, combine ingredients, mixing well. Form into balls and fry in a small amount of oil in a skillet over medium-high heat. (Or if you prefer, put balls on a lightly greased cookie sheet and bake them in the oven at 375° F for 20 to 25 minutes.) Place cooked meatballs in a 9" x 13" baking dish. Cover with a mixture of one can low-fat mushroom soup and one can water. Bake at 350° F for 30 minutes.

PER SERVING

Calories	170
Total Fat	4g
Sat. Fat	0.7g
Cholesterol	0.2mg
Sodium	437mg
Total Carb.	24g
Dietary Fiber	3g
Protein	9g

Quick Oatmeal Patties

Makes 6 patties

1 cup quick oatmeal
1 cup finely-chopped walnuts
2 teaspoons garlic powder
2 teaspoons onion powder

3 tablespoons evaporated milk*
2 eggs*
1/2 teaspoon ground sage
2 tablespoons canola oil (for frying)

In a medium bowl, combine all ingredients—except oil. Shape oatmeal mixture into patties and fry in oil in large skillet over medium-high heat. Place patties in a 9" x 13" baking dish and cover with your favorite sauce or gravy. Bake at 350° F for 30 minutes, or until bubbly.

*LITE VERSION SUBSTITUTION
3 tablespoons evaporated skim milk
1/2 cup egg substitute

PER SERVING	
Calories	308
Total Fat	20g
Sat. Fat	2g
Cholesterol	73mg
Sodium	30mg
Total Carb.	22g
Dietary Fiber	4g
Protein	12g

LITE SERVING	
Calories	297
Total Fat	18g
Sat. Fat	1g
Cholesterol	0.5mg
Sodium	47mg
Total Carb.	22g
Dietary Fiber	4g
Protein	13g

Wheat Germ Patties

JEANNE JARNES

Makes 15 patties

1/4 cup warm water (105° to 115° F)
1 1/2 teaspoons active dry yeast
1/2 teaspoon sugar
1 medium onion, chopped
1 clove garlic, minced
1 1/2 cups wheat germ (raw or toasted)
1 tablespoon soy sauce

2 eggs
1 cup quick oatmeal
1/2 teaspoon ground sage
1 12-ounce can evaporated milk

Sauce:
1 can mushroom soup
1 1/2 cans milk

In a small bowl, combine water, yeast, and sugar. Set aside till foamy.

In a small skillet over medium-high heat, saute onion in 1 tablespoon oil. When tender, add garlic and saute 2 minutes longer. Set aside.

In a large bowl, combine wheat germ, soy sauce, eggs, quick oats, sage, evaporated milk, yeast mixture, and sauteed mixture. Stir well and let stand 5 to 10 minutes. Spray a large skillet with vegetable spray and drop mixture in by spoonfuls; fry on both sides. (This can also be done in the oven on a greased cookie sheet—bake at 350° F for 20 to 30 minutes, turning once.) Arrange patties in a 9" x 13" baking dish.

In a small bowl, combine mushroom soup and milk. Pour over patties. Bake at 350° F for about 30 minutes, or until bubbly.

OPTIONAL: For some crunchiness: add 1/2 cup chopped walnuts to the mixture before frying.

PER SERVING

Calories	129
Total Fat	4g
Sat. Fat	1g
Cholesterol	32mg
Sodium	104mg
Total Carb.	16g
Dietary Fiber	3g
Protein	7g

Baked Macaroni and Cheese

AILEEN ANDRES SOX

Makes 8 servings

2 cups uncooked macaroni
1/4 cup margarine
1/4 cup unbleached white flour
2 cups 1% low-fat milk
1 teaspoon salt

1 teaspoon Wan Jashan® Worcestershire sauce (vegetarian)
1/4 teaspoon dried mustard
1 medium onion, chopped
2 cups grated cheddar cheese

In a medium saucepan, cook macaroni according to package instructions. Drain and set aside.

In a medium saucepan over medium-high heat, melt margarine. Stir in flour to make a paste. Using a wire whisk, slowly add milk. Add salt and whisk while cream sauce thickens. Remove from heat after thickened. Add Worcestershire sauce, dried mustard, onion, and cheese. Stir until mixed.

In a large mixing bowl, combine cooked macaroni and sauce. Stir well. Pour into a square baking dish. Bake at 350° F for about 30 minutes.

OPTIONAL: Sprinkle top with bread crumbs.

PER SERVING

Calories	393
Total Fat	28g
Sat. Fat	15g
Cholesterol	72mg
Sodium	756mg
Total Carb.	16g
Dietary Fiber	1g
Protein	19g

Mom's Macaroni and Cheese

MARION RUNGE

Makes 15 servings

9 cups cooked macaroni
2 cups grated cheddar cheese*
1 teaspoon salt
5 to 6 cups of warm milk
2 eggs*

Cook macaroni according to instructions on package. Drain. Put macaroni and cheddar cheese into a large oblong casserole.

In a large saucepan over medium heat, warm milk and salt. Remove from heat and whisk in eggs. Immediately pour over macaroni and cheese. Bake at 400° F for 35 to 40 minutes.

*LITE VERSION SUBSTITUTION
2 cups grated reduced fat cheddar cheese
1/2 cup egg substitute

PER SERVING	
Calories	293
Total Fat	15g
Sat. Fat	0g
Cholesterol	74mg
Sodium	254mg
Total Carb.	24g
Dietary Fiber	1g
Protein	15g

LITE SERVING	
Calories	183
Total Fat	4g
Sat. Fat	2g
Cholesterol	12mg
Sodium	184mg
Total Carb.	24g
Dietary Fiber	1g
Protein	11g

Macaroni Humor

SUBMITTED BY MARION RUNGE

A church deacon loved this macaroni and cheese dish; however, he was always last in line for potluck, and by the time he got there the dish was always almost empty, leaving little for him. One Sabbath he decided to change that, and he put a note in front of the dish "DO NOT EAT," and nobody did! He had his fill and then the "second helpers" got theirs.

Another Sabbath we had a visitor whose wife presented the special music. When he went through the potluck line, he spied the macaroni dish and helped himself to about a third of the dish and went back to his table to eat it. Those behind him in line gave him a funny look. He came around the second time and finished off the dish. Later his wife apologized to me for his eating so much of it and said that this was his favorite dish, but since his cholesterol level was higher than it ought to be, she quit making it for him at home. He promised me that if I made it again, then he would bring his wife to sing again.

Big Frank Spaghetti

MARTHANNE GLENN

Getting rid of ourself is like peeling an onion, layer by layer, and it is often a tearful process.

Makes 15 servings

Kid Easy

2 26 1/4-ounce cans Franco-American® spaghetti (or 4 14 3/4-ounce cans)
1 20-ounce can Loma Linda Big Franks®, sliced

Dump spaghetti into 9" x 13" baking dish. If desired, cut spaghetti into shorter lengths with a flat-ended spatula for easier eating. Sprinkle sliced Big Franks on top of spaghetti and stir into sauce. Heat in the microwave or oven until bubbly.

A big hit with the kids. Simple, but hey. . .

PER SERVING

Calories	170
Total Fat	19g
Sat. Fat	1g
Cholesterol	3mg
Sodium	724mg
Total Carb.	22g
Dietary Fiber	2g
Protein	10g

Fettuccine With Vegetable Sauce

BARBARA HAMES

Makes 15 servings

3 tablespoons olive oil
3 cloves garlic, minced
1/3 cup pine nuts
6 asparagus spears, fresh or frozen
1 1/2 cups fresh broccoli flowerettes
1 cup sliced fresh zucchini
1 cup frozen petite green peas

10 large mushrooms, sliced
1 medium red pepper, thinly sliced
1/2 teaspoon salt
1 pound fettuccine, uncooked
1/3 cup butter*
1 cup heavy cream*
1/2 cup grated Parmesan cheese*

In a large kettle over medium-high heat, saute garlic and pine nuts in oil for 2 to 3 minutes, or until pine nuts are lightly brown, stirring frequently. Cut fresh asparagus into 1-inch pieces and add with remaining vegetables—except red pepper. Cook, stirring occasionally, until vegetables are crisp-tender (about 5 minutes). Stir in red pepper and salt. Set aside.

In a large kettle over high heat, cook fettuccine. Drain and rinse with cold water; drain well.

In a large saucepan over very low heat, melt butter. Stir in heavy cream and Parmesan cheese. Cook, stirring constantly, until cheese melts. Add pasta and mix well. Gently fold in vegetables. Serve in a casserole dish. *Reheats well.*

*LITE VERSION SUBSTITUTION
Omit butter • 1 12-ounce can evaporated milk • 2 tablespoons grated Parmesan cheese

God seldom speaks to a person while the person is talking.

PER SERVING

Calories	225
Total Fat	13g
Sat. Fat	5g
Cholesterol	47mg
Sodium	204mg
Total Carb.	21g
Dietary Fiber	1g
Protein	7g

LITE SERVING

Calories	167
Total Fat	5g
Sat. Fat	1g
Cholesterol	23mg
Sodium	136mg
Total Carb.	23g
Dietary Fiber	1g
Protein	7g

Lasagna

NATHALIE BISCHOFF

Makes 15 servings

1 1/2 quarts spaghetti sauce
16 ounces low-fat ricotta (or cottage cheese)
1 small zucchini, grated
1/2 pound lasagna noodles, uncooked (or more if needed)
8 ounces low-fat mozzarella cheese, grated

In a large bowl, mix spaghetti sauce, ricotta, and zucchini.

In a 9" x 13" baking dish, spread 1 cup of sauce mixture. Place 2 dry lasagna noodles over sauce. Add more sauce, then noodles. Repeat at least two times. Cover tightly with foil and bake at 350° F for one hour. Bake uncovered 15 more minutes. The last 5 minutes, sprinkle with mozzarella cheese. Let stand 10 to 15 minutes before serving.

VARIATIONS: Firm tofu seasoned with McKay's® Chicken-style Seasoning or 1/2 cup of Loma Linda Vege-Burger® can replace the ricotta. This can be added to the sauce mixture. In place of zucchini you can substitute 1 cup frozen chopped spinach that has been thawed and squeezed dry.

PER SERVING

Calories	174
Total Fat	6g
Sat. Fat	2g
Cholesterol	27mg
Sodium	508g
Total Carb.	17g
Dietary Fiber	1g
Protein	10g

☆One-Step Microwave Lasagna

Makes 8 servings

1 15 1/4-ounce jar spaghetti sauce
1/2 cup water
8 uncooked lasagna noodles
2 cups cottage cheese (large or small curd; low-fat may be substituted)
3 cups grated mozzarella cheese
1/2 cup grated Parmesan cheese

In a medium mixing bowl, combine prepared spaghetti sauce and water. Set aside.

In a 8" x 12" baking dish, spread 1/3 of the spaghetti sauce. Top sauce with 4 lasagna noodles, 1 cup cottage cheese, and 1 cup mozzarella cheese. Spoon 1/2 of remaining sauce over the cheese. Top with remaining 4 noodles, 1 cup cottage cheese, 1 cup mozzarella cheese, and remaining sauce. Sprinkle with Parmesan. Cover with plastic wrap except for one corner.

Microwave at 50% power for 32 to 35 minutes, turning periodically if the microwave does not have a turntable. Sprinkle with remaining 1 cup of mozzarella cheese and microwave uncovered on medium heat for 2 more minutes. Let stand 10 minutes before serving.

This can also be baked in a conventional oven (using foil instead of plastic wrap) at 350° F for 35 to 45 minutes.

Why does everyone want to be in the front of the bus, the rear of the church, and the middle of the road?

PER SERVING

Calories	307
Total Fat	13g
Sat. Fat	7g
Cholesterol	58mg
Sodium	769mg
Total Carb.	23g
Dietary Fiber	1g
Protein	24g

Tetrazzini

SUE STOBUSH

Makes 12 servings

1 12-ounce package spaghetti
1 1/2 cups cottage cheese (large or small curd)*
1 cup sour cream*
1 32-ounce jar spaghetti sauce

1 16-ounce can sliced black olives, drained
1 1/2 cups grated mozzarella cheese*
1 cup grated cheddar cheese*

Cook spaghetti according to package directions. Drain.

In a large bowl, combine cooked spaghetti, cottage cheese, and sour cream. Place in a 9" x 13" baking dish. Pour spaghetti sauce over pasta mixture. Sprinkle olives over sauce. Top with cheeses. Bake at 350° F for 30 to 45 minutes.

*LITE VERSION SUBSTITUTION

1 1/2 cups 1% low-fat cottage cheese (large or small curd)
1 cup fat-free sour cream
1 1/2 cups grated low-fat mozzarella cheese
1 cup grated low-fat cheddar cheese

PER SERVING	
Calories	394
Total Fat	20g
Sat. Fat	10g
Cholesterol	47mg
Sodium	1027mg
Total Carb.	32g
Dietary Fiber	3g
Protein	21g

LITE SERVING	
Calories	345
Total Fat	13g
Sat. Fat	6g
Cholesterol	31mg
Sodium	1142mg
Total Carb.	33g
Dietary Fiber	3g
Protein	22g

Top Ramen Casserole

RUTH DETWILER

FriChik®

Makes 8 servings

2 packages oriental flavor Top Ramen® noodles
2 cups water
1 12-ounce package frozen peas
1 10.75-ounce can cream of mushroom soup
1 8-ounce can sliced water chestnuts
1 12.5-ounce can Worthington FriChik®, diced (reserve liquid)

In a large saucepan over medium-high heat, cook noodles in 2 cups water until tender. Include only one seasoning packet from the Top Ramen noodles. Stir in frozen peas and continue cooking for 2 minutes. Remove from heat. Add mushroom soup, water chestnuts, and FriChik with liquid. Stir well. Pour into a casserole dish and cover with bread crumbs if desired. Bake at 350° F until bubbly.

VARIATIONS TO ADD:

Chopped broccoli
Diced Worthington frozen Smoked Turkey
Celery and onions
Sliced mushrooms
Bac-Os®

PER SERVING	
Calories	234
Total Fat	8g
Sat. Fat	3g
Cholesterol	0.4mg
Sodium	647mg
Total Carb.	30g
Dietary Fiber	4g
Protein	7g

LOW FAT

Tuno Noodle Casserole

Tuno®

Makes 15 servings

1 12-ounce package egg noodles
4 stalks celery, chopped
1/4 cup chopped green pepper
1/4 cup chopped red pepper
1 10.75-ounce can cream of mushroom soup
1 cup 1% low-fat milk
1/2 cup cashew pieces
1 cup fat-free sour cream

1–12 ounce can Worthington Tuno®, drained
   (use 3/4 of a can for a milder flavor)

Topping:
1 cup seasoned bread crumbs
   (cornbread crumbs also work well)
2 tablespoons grated Parmesan cheese

In a large kettle, cook noodles according to package directions. Drain. Pour noodles into large bowl and add all other ingredients—except bread crumbs and Parmesan. Stir well. Pour into 9" x 13" baking dish.

In a small bowl, mix bread crumbs and Parmesan cheese. Sprinkle over noodle mixture. Bake in 350° F for 35 to 40 minutes.

If you like the taste of fish, you will love this recipe. The combination of flavors is wonderful, and the preparation is so easy!

PER SERVING

Calories	211
Total Fat	8g
Sat. Fat	4g
Cholesterol	23mg
Sodium	254mg
Total Carb.	27g
Dietary Fiber	1g
Protein	6g

Johnny Marzetti

Makes 20 servings

2 tablespoons canola oil
1/2 cup diced green pepper
1 cup diced onion
1 cup diced celery
1 15-ounce can tomato sauce
1 16-ounce can tomatoes, chopped and undrained
1 cup water

1 tablespoon sugar
1/2 teaspoon garlic powder
1 4-ounce can sliced mushrooms, drained
1 1/2 cups dehydrated Worthington GranBurger®
8 ounces uncooked egg noodles
8 ounces grated cheddar cheese

In a large skillet over medium-high heat, saute pepper, onion, and celery in oil until tender. Add tomato sauce, tomatoes, water, sugar, garlic powder, mushrooms, and GranBurger. Cover and simmer for 10 to 15 minutes.

Cook egg noodles as package directs. Drain.

In a large mixing bowl, combine noodles and sauce. Place in a 3-quart casserole. Top with cheese and bake uncovered at 350° F for 20 to 30 minutes.

PER SERVING

Calories	145
Total Fat	6g
Sat. Fat	3g
Cholesterol	23mg
Sodium	429mg
Total Carb.	14g
Dietary Fiber	2g
Protein	9g

Worthington Vegetable Steak Stroganoff

CHARLOTTE ISHKANIAN

Makes 8 servings

1 20-ounce can Worthington Vegetable Steaks™, cut into strips and breaded in flour
1 medium onion, chopped
1 6-ounce can sliced mushrooms, drained (or 3/4 cup sliced fresh mushrooms)
1/4 teaspoon garlic powder
2 tablespoons McKay's® Beef-like Seasoning

1/2 teaspoon salt
2 tablespoons soy sauce
1 cup hot water
1 tablespoon dried parsley
2/3 cup sour cream*
1/3 cup grated cheddar cheese*
2 tablespoons canola oil

PER SERVING	
Calories	175
Total Fat	12g
Sat. Fat	5g
Cholesterol	19mg
Sodium	1100mg
Total Carb.	6g
Dietary Fiber	3g
Protein	13g

LITE SERVING	
Calories	117
Total Fat	9g
Sat. Fat	5g
Cholesterol	7mg
Sodium	604mg
Total Carb.	4g
Dietary Fiber	1g
Protein	4g

In a large saucepan over medium-high heat, saute steaks and onion in 2 tablespoons of oil. When onion is tender add mushrooms. Add garlic, seasonings, and water and simmer for 20 minutes or until thickened. Turn heat off and add sour cream and cheese, stirring until cheese is melted.

Pour sauce over cooked noodles of your choice. Rewarm when ready for potluck.

*LITE VERSION SUBSTITUTION

2/3 cup fat-free sour cream • 1/3 cup grated reduced-fat cheddar cheese

HELPFUL HINT: To stretch this recipe (for unexpected company), add additional beef-like seasoning and soy sauce and 1/2 to 1 cup water (in which is dissolved 1 tablespoon cornstarch). Bring to a boil, stirring constantly. Do this before adding cheese and sour cream.

Meatloaf I

Makes 15 servings

1 large onion, diced
1/2 cup canola oil*
1 20-ounce can Worthington Low Fat
  Vegetarian Burger™, crumbled
1 3-ounce package cream cheese, softened
1/2 cup milk*
4 eggs*

2 cups cracker crumbs
1/4 cup ketchup
1 tablespoon prepared mustard
1 tablespoon dried parsley
1 1/2 teaspoons ground sage
1 package G. Washington® Broth

In a large bowl, combine all ingredients. Stir well. Pour into greased 9" x 13" baking dish. Bake at 350° F for 45 minutes.

*LITE VERSION SUBSTITUTION

1/4 cup canola oil
1/2 cup skim milk
1 cup egg substitute

SERVING SUGGESTION: Serve with your favorite gravy or with ketchup.

PER SERVING

Calories	217
Total Fat	12g
Sat. Fat	3g
Cholesterol	64mg
Sodium	327mg
Total Carb.	16g
Dietary Fiber	1g
Protein	10g

LITE SERVING

Calories	163
Total Fat	6g
Sat. Fat	1g
Cholesterol	1mg
Sodium	328mg
Total Carb.	17g
Dietary Fiber	1g
Protein	11g

Meatloaf II

RUTH COLVIN

Don't pray for rain if you are going to complain about the mud.

PER SERVING

Calories	184
Total Fat	12g
Sat. Fat	4g
Cholesterol	60mg
Sodium	510mg
Total Carb.	9g
Dietary Fiber	2g
Protein	11g

LITE SERVING

Calories	157
Total Fat	8g
Sat. Fat	3g
Cholesterol	14mg
Sodium	526mg
Total Carb.	9g
Dietary Fiber	2g
Protein	12g

Makes 15 servings

1/2 cup margarine*
1 large onion, chopped
1/2 pound Velveeta® Lite
   (or 1 8-ounce package cream cheese)*
6 slices whole-wheat bread, cubed

1–20 ounce can Worthington Low Fat
   Vegetarian Burger™, crumbled
1/2 teaspoon ground sage
1/4 teaspoon garlic salt
4 eggs*

In a medium skillet over medium-high heat, saute onion in margarine. Turn heat down and add Velveeta. Stir constantly until cheese has melted. Set aside.

In a large bowl, combine burger, bread, sage, salt, and eggs. Add cheese sauce. Mix well. Pour into a greased 9" x 13" baking dish.

In a small bowl, combine 1/4 cup ketchup, 2 tablespoons water, and 2 tablespoons brown sugar. Pour over meatloaf. Bake at 350° F for 45 minutes.

*LITE VERSION SUBSTITUTION

1/4 cup margarine and 1/4 cup evaporated milk • 1 8-ounce package fat-free cream cheese • 1 cup egg substitute

This meatloaf is soooo good. Leftovers are great for sandwiches because it is so firm, yet moist. A must to try.

Take It to Potluck

SUBMITTED BY EVELYN GLASS

I sampled a vegetarian loaf made from a mix, at the camp meeting display. Thinking it tasted quite good, I bought two packages of the mix.

Later when I served it to my "men folk" they were less than enthusiastic about it! "I'm sorry you don't like it," I said. "The sad thing is I have another package. What will I do with it?"

Without missing a beat, our teenage hired-man said, "Take it to potluck." Which is what I did.

Mushroom Vegeburger Loaf

Makes 15 servings

2 tablespoons canola oil	4 packages G. Washington® Broth
1 large onion, chopped	1 12-ounce can evaporated milk*
1 cup chopped fresh mushrooms	4 eggs*
1 20-ounce can Worthington Low Fat Vegetarian Burger™, crumbled	1 teaspoon ground sage
2 cups grated raw potatoes	1/2 teaspoon ground thyme
	1/2 teaspoon salt

PER SERVING

Calories	128
Total Fat	6g
Sat. Fat	2g
Cholesterol	57mg
Sodium	545mg
Total Carb.	9g
Dietary Fiber	1g
Protein	10g

LITE SERVING

Calories	109
Total Fat	4g
Sat. Fat	0g
Cholesterol	1mg
Sodium	545mg
Total Carb.	9g
Dietary Fiber	1g
Protein	10g

In a small skillet over medium-high heat, saute onion in oil. Set aside.

In a large bowl, combine all other ingredients with sauteed onions. Mix thoroughly. Bake in an ungreased 9" x 13" pan at 350° F for 40 to 45 minutes or until golden brown. Before serving, cover top of loaf with ketchup.

*LITE VERSION SUBSTITUTION

1 12-ounce can evaporated skim milk
1 cup egg substitute

SERVING SUGGESTION: Can be served with your favorite gravy or sauce.

Carrot Roast

Makes 15 servings

3 cups grated carrots
1 1/2 cups corn flakes
1 1/2 cups crushed crackers
1/2 cup chopped walnuts
1 large onion, chopped

1/2 cup grated cheddar cheese
3/4 cup egg substitute (or 3 eggs)
2 cups skim milk
1/2 teaspoon salt
Sage to taste

In a large bowl, combine all ingredients and stir well. Pour into greased 9" x 13" baking dish. Bake at 350° F for 60 minutes. Serve with your favorite gravy.

HELPFUL HINT: Your blender or food processor will come in handy for the chopping in this recipe.

PER SERVING

Calories	148
Total Fat	6g
Sat. Fat	2g
Cholesterol	9mg
Sodium	179mg
Total Carb.	17g
Dietary Fiber	1g
Protein	7g

Cottage Cheese Roast (with Rice Krispies)

Sue White

Makes 8 servings

1/2 cup margarine*
1 large onion, chopped
6 cups Rice Krispies® cereal
4 eggs*
1 quart (4 cups) cottage cheese (large or small curd)*
3 packages G. Washington® Broth

In a medium-sized skillet, saute onion in margarine. Set aside.

In a large bowl, combine Rice Krispies, eggs, cottage cheese, GWB, and sauteed onions. Stir well and pour into greased 9" x 13" baking dish. Bake at 350° F for 45 minutes.

*Lite Version Substitution

1/4 cup margarine and 1/4 cup evaporated milk
1 cup egg substitute
1 quart (4 cups) 1% low-fat cottage cheese (large or small curd)

What could be easier? Serve with a favorite gravy.

PER SERVING	
Calories	361
Total Fat	19g
Sat. Fat	6g
Cholesterol	123mg
Sodium	670mg
Total Carb.	27g
Dietary Fiber	0.7g
Protein	19g

LITE SERVING	
Calories	272
Total Fat	1g
Sat. Fat	2g
Cholesterol	5mg
Sodium	670mg
Total Carb.	28g
Dietary Fiber	0.7g
Protein	20g

Lentil Roast

Makes 15 servings

2 cups cooked lentils
1 12-ounce can evaporated milk*
2 tablespoons canola oil
1 1/2 cups bread crumbs, crushed corn flakes,
  or Special K® cereal
1 egg*

1 cup chopped walnuts
1 teaspoon salt
1/2 teaspoon ground sage
1 medium onion, chopped
1 cup grated carrots
1 cup finely-chopped celery

In a large bowl, combine all ingredients—including lentils—and mix thoroughly. Pour into greased 9" x 13" baking dish. Bake at 350° F for one hour.

*LITE VERSION SUBSTITUTION

1 12-ounce can evaporated skim milk
1/4 cup egg substitute

SERVING SUGGESTION: Serve with your favorite sauce or gravy.

PER SERVING	
Calories	185
Total Fat	9g
Sat. Fat	2g
Cholesterol	21mg
Sodium	289mg
Total Carb.	18g
Dietary Fiber	3g
Protein	8g

LITE SERVING	
Calories	172
Total Fat	7g
Sat. Fat	0.7g
Cholesterol	1mg
Sodium	297mg
Total Carb.	19g
Dietary Fiber	3g
Protein	9g

Mock Turkey Roast I

Makes 15 servings

1 20-ounce can Worthington Vegetable Skallops®, ground
1 medium onion, finely chopped
2 cups Pepperidge Farm® Herb Stuffing, finely ground

1/4 cup canola oil
3 eggs*
1 cup milk*
1 cup grated cheddar cheese*
1 tablespoon dried sweet basil

In a large bowl, mix together all ingredients. Pour into a greased 9" x 13" baking dish. Bake at 350° F for one hour.

*LITE VERSION SUBSTITUTION

3/4 cup egg substitute
1 cup skim milk
1 cup grated low-fat cheddar cheese

PER SERVING

Calories	177
Total Fat	11g
Sat. Fat	5g
Cholesterol	56mg
Sodium	349mg
Total Carb.	8g
Dietary Fiber	1g
Protein	11g

LITE SERVING

Calories	128
Total Fat	6g
Sat. Fat	2g
Cholesterol	6mg
Sodium	324mg
Total Carb.	8g
Dietary Fiber	1g
Protein	9g

Mock Turkey Roast II

SYLVIA YTEBERG

Makes 15 servings

1 20-ounce can Worthington Low Fat
  Vegetarian Burger™, crumbled
1 large onion, diced
2 cups cracker crumbs
1/2 cup canola oil*

1 teaspoon poultry seasoning
3/4 cup milk
3/4 teaspoon salt
1 8-ounce package cream cheese, softened*
2 eggs*

In a large bowl, mix all ingredients together. Pour into a greased 9" x 13" baking dish. Bake at 350° F for one hour.

*LITE VERSION SUBSTITUTION

Omit oil
1 8-ounce package fat-free cream cheese
1/2 cup egg substitute

PER SERVING	
Calories	252
Total Fat	15g
Sat. Fat	5g
Cholesterol	46mg
Sodium	434mg
Total Carb.	17g
Dietary Fiber	1g
Protein	12g

LITE SERVING	
Calories	130
Total Fat	2g
Sat. Fat	0g
Cholesterol	3mg
Sodium	397
Total Carb.	16g
Dietary Fiber	1g
Protein	11g

Potato Roast

AILEEN ANDRES SOX

Vita-Burger®

Makes 12 servings

1/2 cup boiling water
1/2 cup dry Loma Linda Vita-Burger®
1 cup grated cheddar cheese*
3 cups frozen hash brown potatoes
 (or 3 cups grated potatoes)

1 10.75-ounce can cream of mushroom soup
3 eggs*
1/2 cup chopped onion

In a small bowl, add Vita-Burger to boiling water. Let soak while preparing other ingredients.

In a large bowl, combine all ingredients—including Vita-Burger—and pour into a greased 9" x 13" baking dish. Bake at 350° F for one hour.

*LITE VERSION SUBSTITUTION

1 cup grated low-fat cheddar cheese
3/4 cup egg substitute

PER SERVING	
Calories	201
Total Fat	13g
Sat. Fat	6g
Cholesterol	68mg
Sodium	327mg
Total Carb.	12g
Dietary Fiber	1g
Protein	8g

LITE SERVING	
Calories	146
Total Fat	8g
Sat. Fat	3g
Cholesterol	7mg
Sodium	295mg
Total Carb.	12g
Dietary Fiber	1g
Protein	6g

Choplet Casserole

Makes 8 servings

Choplets®

1 20-ounce can Worthington Choplets®, drained
(reserve liquid)
1 medium onion, chopped
2 tablespoons canola oil
2 tablespoons flour
2 cups cold water

1 package G. Washington® Broth
1 tablespoon Vegex® (or 1 cube Maggi® Vegetarian
Vegetable Bouillon)
1/2 cup diced green pepper
1 large tomato, chopped
1 4-ounce can sliced mushrooms (with liquid)

Dip each Choplet in flour and fry in a large skillet sprayed with vegetable spray over medium-high heat, browning both sides. Put into 8" square baking dish.

In the same skillet, saute onion in 2 tablespoons of oil until tender. Add flour and stir well. Add Choplet liquid and water and stir until smooth. *You may not need the entire 2 cups of water.* Add seasonings, green pepper, tomato, and mushrooms (with liquid). Cover Choplets with sauce mixture. Bake at 350° F for about 1/2 hour. The liquid will be absorbed by the Choplets and the Choplets will swell and become very tender.

PER SERVING

Calories	98
Total Fat	4g
Sat. Fat	1g
Cholesterol	0mg
Sodium	431mg
Total Carb.	7g
Dietary Fiber	2g
Protein	4g

Hot Chicken Salad

Makes 20 servings

Meatless
Chicken

4 cups sliced celery
2 cups chopped onion
4 cups diced Worthington frozen Meatless Chicken
2 cups cooked white or brown rice
1 4-ounce can sliced mushrooms
2 teaspoons McKay's® Chicken-style Seasoning

1 1/2 cups mayonnaise*
1 cup sliced almonds*

Topping:
4 cups crushed cornflakes
3 tablespoons margarine, melted
1 cup grated cheddar cheese

PER SERVING

Calories	303
Total Fat	23g
Sat. Fat	6g
Cholesterol	22mg
Sodium	417mg
Total Carb.	14g
Dietary Fiber	2g
Protein	10g

LITE SERVING

Calories	175
Total Fat	8g
Sat. Fat	3g
Cholesterol	13mg
Sodium	427mg
Total Carb.	15g
Dietary Fiber	2g
Protein	9g

In a large skillet, water saute** celery and onion. Set aside.

In a large bowl, combine chicken, rice, mushrooms, seasoning, mayonnaise, almonds, and sauteed mixture. Mix well. Pour into greased 9" x 13" baking dish and bake at 350° F for 45 minutes.

In a medium mixing bowl, mix crushed cornflakes, margarine, and cheese. During the last 10 minutes of baking, sprinkle cornflake topping over the top of casserole. Bake for 10 more minutes. Serve hot.

*LITE VERSION SUBSTITUTION
1 1/2 cups fat-free Miracle Whip® (or mayonnaise)
Omit sliced almonds

This is great for special occasions.

**Simmer vegetables in just enough water to keep covered—until tender.

Kraut and Big Frank Casserole

JUDY ANDERSON

Big Franks

Makes 10 servings

1 20-ounce can Loma Linda Big Franks®, sliced
3 cups drained sauerkraut
1 10.75-ounce can cream of mushroom soup
1 cup mayonnaise*
6 medium potatoes, boiled and diced

In a large bowl, mix all ingredients—except potatoes. Place hot potatoes in bottom of a 9" x 13" baking dish. Add sauerkraut mixture. If desired, sprinkle with bread crumbs or crushed potato chips. Bake at 350° F for 30 minutes.

*LITE VERSION SUBSTITUTION
1 cup fat-free Miracle Whip® (or mayonnaise)

PER SERVING

Calories	290
Total Fat	16g
Sat. Fat	3g
Cholesterol	6mg
Sodium	855mg
Total Carb.	28g
Dietary Fiber	4g
Protein	11g

LITE SERVING

Calories	222
Total Fat	8g
Sat. Fat	2g
Cholesterol	0mg
Sodium	888mg
Total Carb.	28g
Dietary Fiber	4g
Protein	10g

Spinach-Scalloped Franks

Big Franks

Makes 15 servings

1 10-ounce package frozen chopped spinach,
  cooked and drained
6 tablespoons margarine
1/2 cup chopped onion
1/4 cup unbleached white flour
1 1/2 cups skim milk

2 cups grated cheddar cheese
5 cups boiled, pared, and sliced potatoes
  (about five medium)
1 20-ounce can Loma Linda Big Franks®,
  Worthington Veja-Links® or Linketts®, sliced

Cook spinach according to package directions. After cooking, drain well.

In a medium saucepan over medium-high heat, saute onion in margarine. Add flour to make a paste. Slowly add milk and whisk with wire whisk, stirring constantly until thickened. Add 1 1/2 cups of the cheese to the white sauce. Stir in drained spinach. Set aside.

Arrange 1/2 of the sliced potatoes in a 9" x 13" baking dish. Top with 1/2 of the sliced links and 1/2 of the spinach mixture. Repeat, ending with spinach mixture. Top with remaining 1/2 cup of cheese. Bake at 350° F for 40 to 50 minutes.

PER SERVING

Calories	298
Total Fat	19g
Sat. Fat	8g
Cholesterol	35mg
Sodium	387mg
Total Carb.	16g
Dietary Fiber	3g
Protein	16g

Tater Tot Casserole

BECKY OWENS

FriChik®

Makes 10 servings

2 tablespoons margarine
1 medium onion, chopped
2 stalks celery, diced
1 12.5-ounce can Worthington FriChik®, diced
  (reserve liquid)

1 10.75-ounce cream of mushroom soup
1 cup grated cheddar cheese
1 32-ounce bag frozen Ore-Ida Tater Tots®

In a large skillet over medium-high heat, saute onion and celery in margarine till tender. Add diced FriChik (with liquid), soup, and cheese; stir until well blended. Thin mixture with a soup-can of water. Add Tater Tots and mix well. Place in a one-quart casserole dish and cover. Bake at 350° F for one hour.

Bibles that are coming apart usually belong to people who are not.

PER SERVING	
Calories	310
Total Fat	18g
Sat. Fat	6g
Cholesterol	21mg
Sodium	438mg
Total Carb.	27g
Dietary Fiber	3g
Protein	11g

Tortilla Burger Casserole

JEANNE JARNES

Low Fat
Vegetarian
Burger

Makes 15 servings

1 large onion, chopped
1 20-ounce can Worthington Low Fat
   Vegetarian Burger™, crumbled
1 10.75-ounce can tomato soup
1 15-ounce can tomato sauce

1 15-ounce can water
1 package taco seasoning
1 dozen corn tortillas, torn into bite-sized pieces
1 16-ounce can sliced black olives, drained
1 cup grated cheddar cheese (optional)

In a large skillet over medium-high heat, water-saute* onion. Add crumbled burger, tomato soup, tomato sauce, water, taco seasoning, and black olives.

In a 9" x 13" baking dish, layer torn tortillas and sauce ending with cheese. Bake at 350° F until bubbly (35 to 45 minutes). Serve with a dollop of fat-free sour cream, if desired.

Leave off the cheese topping to cut down on calories and cholesterol.

*Simmer onion in just enough water to keep covered—until tender.

Vegetarian Chili Tamale Casserole

DIAN LAWRENCE

Spicy Chili

Makes 20 servings

3 20-ounce cans Natural Touch Spicy Chili
2 12-ounce cans whole kernel corn, drained
1 large green pepper, chopped
2 tablespoons chili powder
1 teaspoon garlic powder

1/2 teaspoon ground cumin
1 cup ketchup
Crust:
1 16-ounce can Marie Callender's Corn Bread Mix
1 1/2 cups water

In a large saucepan over medium-high heat, combine chili, corn, pepper, seasonings, and ketchup. Cook until hot, stirring often.

Spray a 9" x 13" baking dish with vegetable spray. Pour chili mixture into baking dish.

Prepare corn bread mix according to package directions. Drop by spoonfuls on top of casserole. Mixture spreads so do not try to cover casserole completely. Bake in 400° F oven for 25 to 30 minutes or until crust is golden brown.

People always ask for this recipe.

PER SERVING	
Calories	215
Total Fat	3g
Sat. Fat	0g
Cholesterol	15mg
Sodium	765mg
Total Carb.	37g
Dietary Fiber	6g
Protein	10g

Hot Potluck

SUBMITTED BY CHAR DASSENKO

In my little church we have a potluck dinner once a month. We have three Hispanic families who attend church and bring food to our potlucks. I am not much for spicy food, so I usually pass up these dishes.

One Sabbath, however, the pastor talked me into trying some. He said it was really good and not even spicy. As soon as I put the first forkful into my mouth and started chewing it, I cried "WOW!"

Now I must be extra gullible, or maybe they just do a great job of teaching persuasion at the seminary. Even while the pastor was laughing at me, he talked me into trying another mouthful. That mouthful was hotter than the first! I had to hurry and get a drink of water. But at least our hard-working pastor got a good laugh.

Corn Tamale Pie

Ann Thrash-Trumbo

Makes 8 servings

2 1/2 cups liquid (juice from canned tomatoes + water)
1 cup yellow cornmeal
2 cups whole kernel corn, drained
3/4 cup sliced black olives
1 cup chopped onion

3 cups canned tomatoes, drained (reserve juice)
1 teaspoon salt
1 teaspoon dried basil
1 teaspoon garlic powder
1 teaspoon dried Italian seasoning

In a medium saucepan over medium-high heat, bring tomato liquid to a boil. Whisk in corn meal. *This must be done very briskly or it will form lumps.*

In a medium skillet over medium-high heat, simmer remaining ingredients until onion starts to become transparent.

Place cornmeal mixture in a 9" x 13" baking dish, forming a thick pie crust with raised edges. Pour the corn-tomato mixture into the crust. Bake at 350° F for 1 hour.

HEALTHY CHOICE

Better a meal of vegetables where there is love than a fattened calf with hatred.

PROVERBS 15:17, NIV

PER SERVING

Calories	135
Total Fat	3g
Sat. Fat	0.4g
Cholesterol	0mg
Sodium	774mg
Total Carb.	26g
Dietary Fiber	4g
Protein	4g

Tamale Pie

Makes 10 servings

1/2 cup canola oil
1 medium onion, chopped
1 16-ounce can tomatoes, drained and chopped
1 cup whole kernel corn (frozen or canned)
1 teaspoon salt

1 cup skim milk
1 1/2 cups yellow cornmeal
1 16-ounce can sliced black olives, drained
3 eggs (or 3/4 cup egg substitute)
2 teaspoons chili powder

In a large kettle over medium-high heat, saute onion in oil until tender. Add all other ingredients in order, stirring well. *This mixture will thicken but tends to scorch easily, so stir constantly until thickened.* Pour into a well-greased bread or loaf pan. Bake at 375° F for 35 to 45 minutes or until top is golden brown.

SERVING SUGGESTION: This loaf can be turned out onto a platter and and garnished with parsley.

PER SERVING

Calories	255
Total Fat	16g
Sat. Fat	2g
Cholesterol	56mg
Sodium	783mg
Total Carb.	24g
Dietary Fiber	3g
Protein	5g

Microwaved Tortilla Pie

Makes 8 servings

6 medium-sized flour tortillas
1 cup chopped fresh tomato
1/2 cup chopped onion
1 4-ounce can diced green chilies, drained
1 cup sliced black olives
1/2 cup grated cheddar cheese*

1/2 cup grated Monterey Jack cheese*
3 eggs*
3/4 cup milk*
1/2 teaspoon chili powder
1/4 teaspoon salt

Line a well-greased quiche pan and sides with tortillas. Top with tomato, onion, chilies, black olives, and cheeses.

In a medium bowl, combine eggs, milk, chili powder, and salt, beating well. Pour into lined pan. On medium heat, microwave for eight minutes, giving dish a half-turn halfway through. Then cook for another ten minutes or until knife inserted in the middle comes out clean.

Just rewarm when ready to serve. *Great with taco or picante sauce.*

*LITE VERSION SUBSTITUTION

1/2 cup grated reduced-fat cheddar cheese
1/2 cup grated reduced-fat Monterey Jack cheese
3/4 cup egg substitute
3/4 cup skim milk

PER SERVING

Calories	185
Total Fat	9g
Sat. Fat	4g
Cholesterol	84mg
Sodium	650mg
Total Carb.	17g
Dietary Fiber	2g
Protein	9g

LITE SERVING

Calories	171
Total Fat	7g
Sat. Fat	2g
Cholesterol	10mg
Sodium	708mg
Total Carb.	17g
Dietary Fiber	2g
Protein	9g

Moist Bread Stuffing

Makes 15 servings

Meatless Chicken

1 cup margarine
8 stalks celery, finely sliced
1 1/2 cups finely-chopped onions
1/4 cup finely-chopped fresh parsley
1 cup warm water

2 tablespoons McKay's® Chicken-style Seasoning
8 cups cubed day-old bread
3 eggs
Worthington frozen Meatless Chicken slices, thawed
(optional)

In a large kettle over medium-high heat, melt margarine. Saute celery and onions until tender. Add parsley, water, McKay's Chicken-style Seasoning, bread cubes, and eggs. Mix well. Pour into greased 9" x 13" baking dish. If desired, place Worthington Meatless Chicken slices on top before baking. Bake at 350° F for 30 to 40 minutes.

PER SERVING

Calories	196
Total Fat	14g
Sat. Fat	3g
Cholesterol	37mg
Sodium	498mg
Total Carb.	14g
Dietary Fiber	1g
Protein	4g

Athenian Rice With Feta Cheese

Makes 8 servings

1 tablespoon olive oil
1 cup chopped red onion
1 cup chopped red bell pepper
1 garlic clove, minced
3 cups cooked brown rice

1/2 cup sun-dried tomatoes, cut into strips (optional)
1 4 1/2-ounce can sliced black olives, drained
1 tablespoon finely-chopped fresh parsley
1 1/2 teaspoons dried oregano leaves
1/2 cup crumbled feta cheese

In a large skillet over medium-high heat, saute onion, red pepper, and garlic in oil; stir until onion is tender. Stir in rice, sun-dried tomatoes, olives, parsley, and oregano. Heat thoroughly. Remove from heat and add feta cheese. Stir well. Cool and store in refrigerator until ready to serve.

To warm up simply put in a glass serving bowl and microwave until heated thoroughly.

PER SERVING

Calories	154
Total Fat	5g
Sat. Fat	2g
Cholesterol	8mg
Sodium	307mg
Total Carb.	23g
Dietary Fiber	3g
Protein	4g

Chicken Curry

BECKY OWENS

would be good & Potatoes too

FriChik®

Makes 8 servings

1 tablespoon margarine*
1 medium onion, chopped
2 eggs*
1 10.75-ounce can cream of mushroom soup
1 12-ounce can evaporated milk*

1 12.5-ounce can Worthington FriChik®, diced (with liquid)
1 cup frozen peas *or canned*
1 tablespoon curry powder

In a large skillet over medium-high heat, saute onion in margarine until tender. Crack eggs into onion mixture, frying until dry, stirring constantly. Add mushroom soup and evaporated milk, stirring until creamy. Add FriChik (with liquid) to sauce mixture, followed by peas and curry powder. Simmer gently until peas are cooked. Serve over rice; preferably basmati.

*LITE VERSION SUBSTITUTION

Water (just enough to keep onions in skillet covered)
4 ounces firm tofu, diced
1 12-ounce can evaporated skim milk or non-dairy milk substitute

In a large skillet over medium-high heat, saute onion in water. When onions are tender and water is evaporated, add tofu, mushroom soup, and evaporated milk, stirring until creamy. Add FriChik (with liquid) and proceed as above.

Company Chicken

NANCY KYTE

FriChik®

Makes 8 servings

1 10-ounce jar apricot jam
1/2 cup Catalina (or Russian) salad dressing
1 package dehydrated Lipton® Onion Soup Mix
1/4 cup mayonnaise
3 12.5-ounce cans whole Worthington FriChik®, drained

In a medium bowl, whisk together jam, salad dressing, soup mix, and mayonnaise.

In a 8" x 12" baking dish, arrange FriChik pieces. Cover FriChik with sauce. Bake at 350° F for 30 to 40 minutes, or until bubbly.

*LITE VERSION SUBSTITUTION

1 10-ounce jar reduced-calorie apricot jam
1/2 cup fat-free Catalina salad dressing
1/4 cup fat-free Miracle Whip® (or mayonnaise)

LITE SERVING

Calories	237
Total Fat	2g
Sat. Fat	1g
Cholesterol	0.2mg
Sodium	1077mg
Total Carb.	31g
Dietary Fiber	2g
Protein	10g

Sam's Fried Chicken

SHIRLEY JUHL

Makes 20 servings

2 large rolls Worthington frozen Chic-Ketts®, thawed
1 quart cultured buttermilk, from skim milk
2 cups unbleached white flour
1 cup yellow cornmeal
2 teaspoons garlic powder (or to taste)

Tartar sauce:

1 cup fat-free Miracle Whip®
2 tablespoons sweet pickle relish
1 tablespoon chopped onion

Thaw Chic-Ketts and tear into medium-sized chunks. Pour buttermilk over torn Chic-Ketts until covered completely. (You may not have to use all the buttermilk.) This can sit for up to one week before frying.

In gallon zip-lock bag, mix flour, cornmeal and garlic powder. Drain Chic-Ketts (do not save the buttermilk—it doesn't taste the same). Drop small portions into zip-lock bag and shake until thoroughly coated. Best if fried immediately in a deep-fat fryer until golden. Serve hot or cold with tartar sauce.

Please note: the nutritional figures are out of proportion due to the amount of buttermilk used for soaking the Chic-Ketts. In actuality, only around 1/4 to 1/2 cup buttermilk is used.

PER SERVING

Calories	163
Total Fat	6g
Sat. Fat	1g
Cholesterol	0mg
Sodium	476mg
Total Carb.	16g
Dietary Fiber	2g
Protein	12g

Garden Pizza

KAREN STAPLES

Makes 20 servings

1 Chicago Pizza Crust Recipe (see p. 25)
  (nutritional analysis includes the crust)
1 8-ounce package fat-free cream cheese, softened
1/2 cup fat-free Miracle Whip® (or mayonnaise)
1 clove garlic, crushed

1 pound tomatoes, chopped
1/2 pound cucumbers, chopped
1 medium onion, chopped
1 4-ounce can mushrooms, drained
1 16-ounce can sliced black olives, drained

After Chicago Pizza Crust dough has raised, spread with fingers onto a large, greased cookie sheet. You may not need all the dough, depending on how thick you like it. Prick with a fork before baking. Bake at 350° F for 10 to 15 minutes, or until golden. Remove and cool.

In a medium bowl, beat cream cheese, mayonnaise, and garlic together until smooth. Spread over cooled pizza crust. Chop any toppings you like (some examples are listed) and sprinkle over cream cheese mixture. Top with olives. Keep in refrigerator until ready to serve.

This is great for a summer potluck, especially if the church is going to a park! You will find it so refreshing.

HEALTHY CHOICE

PER SERVING

Calories	154
Total Fat	5g
Sat. Fat	0.6g
Cholesterol	0mg
Sodium	703mg
Total Carb.	23g
Dietary Fiber	2g
Protein	4g

Morningstar Farms Sausage and Spinach Quiche

Makes 12 servings

Breakfast
Patties

1 prepared pie crust
1 1/2 cups grated low-fat Swiss cheese
4 frozen Morningstar Farms Breakfast Patties,
   thawed and crumbled
1/2 cup Pepperidge Farm® bread stuffing mix

1/2 of a 10-ounce package frozen chopped spinach,
   thawed and drained
3/4 cup egg substitute
1 1/2 cups skim milk

Sprinkle Swiss cheese on bottom of pie shell. Top with crumbled patties, stuffing mix, and spinach.

In a medium bowl, combine eggs and milk. Beat well and pour over sausage mixture. Bake uncovered at 325° F for 50 to 55 minutes or until a knife inserted in the center of the pie comes out clean. Let stand 10 minutes before cutting.

This usually makes 8 generous servings, but for potluck I cut smaller. Very colorful and the flavor is divine. And yes, real men do eat quiche.

PER SERVING

Calories	104
Total Fat	5g
Sat. Fat	2g
Cholesterol	11mg
Sodium	200mg
Total Carb.	5g
Dietary Fiber	1g
Protein	11g

SECTION 5

Vegetables

Baked Corn

CARLENE BAUGHER

Makes 8 servings

2 16-ounce cans cream-style corn
2 eggs (or 1/2 cup egg substitute)
2 tablespoons sugar
2 tablespoons flour
6 1/2 ounces evaporated milk
2 tablespoons chopped red pepper
2 tablespoons chopped green pepper

In a medium bowl, mix all ingredients. Pour into greased 9" x 13" baking dish. Bake at 350° F for one hour. Serve hot. *This can be rewarmed.*

PER SERVING

Calories	146
Total Fat	3g
Sat. Fat	1g
Cholesterol	53mg
Sodium	407mg
Total Carb.	26g
Dietary Fiber	2g
Protein	5g

Blender-Grated Potato Casserole

JUDY WENDT

Makes 8 servings

1 cup 1% low-fat milk*

3 eggs*

1 1/2 teaspoons salt

1 cup cubed cheddar cheese*

1 tablespoon dried parsley

1 small onion, quartered

4 medium potatoes, cubed

Put ingredients in blender in order listed. Cover blender and run on high just until potatoes are bite-sized pieces. Pour mixture into a lightly greased casserole dish. Bake at 350° F for 1 hour.

Can't be easier than that!

*LITE VERSION SUBSTITUTION

1 cup skim milk

3/4 cups egg substitute

1 cup cubed reduced fat cheddar cheese

PER SERVING	
Calories	212
Total Fat	12g
Sat. Fat	7g
Cholesterol	103mg
Sodium	666mg
Total Carb.	14g
Dietary Fiber	1g
Protein	12g

LITE SERVING	
Calories	172
Total Fat	7g
Sat. Fat	3g
Cholesterol	21mg
Sodium	738mg
Total Carb.	13g
Dietary Fiber	1g
Protein	12g

Broccoli-Swiss Cheese Casserole

Breakfast Strips

Makes 8 servings

1/4 cup water
3 cups fresh broccoli flowerettes
1/4 cup chopped onion
1 cup whole corn (frozen or canned)
1/2 cup grated Swiss cheese*
1 tablespoon margarine
2 cups cottage cheese (large or small curd)*

2 eggs*
1/4 cup unbleached white flour
1/4 teaspoon salt
4 dashes hot sauce
8 slices uncooked Morningstar Farms Breakfast Strips®, cut into small pieces
1/3 cup seasoned dried bread crumbs

PER SERVING	
Calories	189
Total Fat	8g
Sat. Fat	2g
Cholesterol	57mg
Sodium	640mg
Total Carb.	16g
Dietary Fiber	3g
Protein	15g

LITE SERVING	
Calories	167
Total Fat	8g
Sat. Fat	2g
Cholesterol	5mg
Sodium	309mg
Total Carb.	14g
Dietary Fiber	2g
Protein	13g

In a large saucepan over medium-high heat, cook broccoli and onion in water until tender but crisp. Drain.

In a large bowl, combine broccoli and onions, corn, and Swiss cheese. Stir.

In blender put margarine, cottage cheese, eggs, flour, salt, and hot sauce; blend till smooth. Pour over vegetable mixture. Stir till mixed. Pour into square baking dish. Bake in microwave or 350° F oven till bubbly.

Combine bread crumbs and Breakfast Strips and sprinkle on top. Bake a few minutes longer.

*LITE VERSION SUBSTITUTION:
1/2 cup grated reduced-fat Swiss cheese • 12 ounces firm tofu, drained and crumbled • 1/2 cup egg substitute

Carrot Ring

Makes 8 servings

2 cups grated carrots
1 tablespoon grated onion
1 cup skim milk
1 teaspoon granulated sugar
1 teaspoon salt

2 tablespoons margarine
2 tablespoons flour
3 eggs
1/4 cup finely-chopped fresh parsley

In a large bowl, mix all ingredients. Pour into greased ring baking mold. Set in a pan of water and place in oven. Bake at 300° F for about 1 hour or until firm.

SERVING SUGGESTION: After turning the ring onto a platter and unmolding, put cooked, frozen green peas in the center.

Very colorful.

PER SERVING

Calories	83
Total Fat	4g
Sat. Fat	1g
Cholesterol	70mg
Sodium	364mg
Total Carb.	7g
Dietary Fiber	1g
Protein	4g

Curried Potatoes

JUDY ANDERSON

Makes 10 servings

6 medium-sized potatoes
6 eggs*
2 cups sour cream*
1/2 cup butter, melted

1 1/2 teaspoons salt
2 teaspoons curry powder
1 10.75-ounce can cream of mushroom soup

PER SERVING	
Calories	320
Total Fat	23g
Sat. Fat	13g
Cholesterol	117mg
Sodium	703mg
Total Carb.	23g
Dietary Fiber	2g
Protein	6g

LITE SERVING	
Calories	217
Total Fat	12g
Sat. Fat	6g
Cholesterol	21mg
Sodium	594mg
Total Carb.	24g
Dietary Fiber	2g
Protein	4g

In a large kettle over medium-high heat, boil potatoes and eggs. Remove eggs after 7 minutes of boiling. Continue boiling potatoes until tender. Remove from heat. When cool, remove skins from potatoes and shells from eggs. Grate potatoes and chop eggs.

In a medium bowl, combine sour cream, butter, salt, curry powder, and mushroom soup. Set aside.

In a greased 9" x 13" baking dish, layer grated potatoes, eggs, and sour cream mixture. Bake at 325° F for 30 minutes.

*LITE VERSION SUBSTITUTION

Omit eggs
2 cups fat-free sour cream
Add 1/2 cup skim milk (to mushroom soup mixture)

OPTIONAL: Top with buttered bread crumbs prior to baking.

Eggplant Patties

Blanche Fisher

Makes 6 patties

1 tablespoon canola oil	1/2 teaspoon salt
1/2 cup finely-chopped onion	1 tablespoon finely-chopped green pepper
2 cups cubed eggplant	1/2 cup old-fashioned rolled oats
1/2 cup cracker crumbs	

In a small skillet, saute onion in oil. Set aside.

In a medium saucepan, boil eggplant in a small amount of water until tender. Drain.

In a medium bowl, mix eggplant, onion, and the rest of the ingredients. Form into small patties and brown on both sides in small amount of oil.

These are excellent in sandwiches.

PER SERVING

Calories	119
Total Fat	3g
Sat. Fat	0.4g
Cholesterol	0mg
Sodium	198mg
Total Carb.	19g
Dietary Fiber	2g
Protein	3g

Haricots Verts Almandine*

CORRINE VANDERWERFF

Makes 8 servings

2 pounds green beans, ends trimmed, cut into 1" pieces
1/4 cup margarine
1 1/3 cups thinly sliced onion
6 tablespoons slivered almonds

In large kettle over medium-high heat, cook green beans in a small amount of water. Drain and set aside.

In a small skillet over medium-high heat, saute onions and almonds in margarine until almonds are golden and onions are tender.

Place beans in a glass serving dish and top with onions and almonds. *This reheats well in the oven.*

PER SERVING

Calories	122
Total Fat	8g
Sat. Fat	1g
Cholesterol	0mg
Sodium	8mg
Total Carb.	11g
Dietary Fiber	5g
Protein	3g

*French for "green beans garnished with almonds"

Lima Bean Paisano

Stripples®

Makes 15 servings

3 10-ounce packages frozen baby Lima beans
1 tablespoon canola oil
1 cup sliced onion
3 tablespoons flour
1/2 cup sour cream

1 0.7-ounce package Good Seasons® Italian-style
  Salad Dressing Mix
1/2 teaspoon dried oregano leaves
1 cup grated mozzarella cheese
4 slices Worthington Stripples®, cut into pieces

Cook Lima beans as package directs; drain, reserving 2/3 cup liquid. Set aside.

In a small skillet over medium heat, saute onion in oil till tender. Stir in flour to make a smooth paste; blend in 2/3 cup reserved cooking liquid. Cook, stirring until thickened and smooth. Remove from heat.

In a large bowl, combine Lima beans, sauce, sour cream, dressing mix, and oregano.

Pour 1/3 Lima bean mixture into a 2-quart casserole. Top with 1/3 of the cheese. Repeat twice. Top with Worthington Stripples pieces. Bake covered at 350° F for 30 minutes; uncovered for 10 minutes longer.

PER SERVING

Calories	262
Total Fat	5g
Sat. Fat	2g
Cholesterol	12mg
Sodium	102mg
Total Carb.	38g
Dietary Fiber	12g
Protein	16g

Nepalese Curried Vegetables

CELESTE PERRINO WALKER

Makes 8 servings

2 tablespoons canola oil
1 whole garlic bulb, separated into cloves*, skins removed
2 medium onions, chopped
1 tablespoon curry powder
1 cerrano chile, cut lengthwise

1 cup water
2 cups chopped fresh cauliflower
2 cups sliced carrots
2 medium potatoes, cubed
1 cup frozen peas
1 teaspoon salt (optional)

In a large skillet, saute onions and garlic in oil until translucent. Add curry powder. Stir in chile. Add water, cauliflower, carrots, potatoes, peas, and salt (if desired.) Continue to cook until vegetables are tender, adding more water if necessary. When vegetables are done, spoon over cooked Basmati** rice.

PER SERVING

Calories	170
Total Fat	4g
Sat. Fat	0.4g
Cholesterol	0mg
Sodium	26mg
Total Carb.	27g
Dietary Fiber	9g
Protein	8g

* Yes! One whole garlic bulb!
** An Indian rice with a very fragrant flavor—found in your local grocery store.

☆Orange-Glazed Sweet Potatoes Royale

Makes 12 servings

2 16-ounce cans sweet potatoes, drained
1 cup brown sugar
2 tablespoons cornstarch
1/2 teaspoon salt
2 cups orange juice

1/3 cup raisins
1/4 cup water
1 teaspoon orange zest
Walnut halves (optional)

In a 9" x 13" baking dish, arrange drained sweet potatoes.

In a medium saucepan, mix sugar, cornstarch, and salt; blend in orange juice; add raisins. Cook over medium-high heat until boiling. Add remaining ingredients. Pour over sweet potatoes. Garnish with halved walnuts if desired. Bake uncovered at 350° F for 25 to 30 minutes.

PER SERVING

Calories	150
Total Fat	0.3g
Sat. Fat	0g
Cholesterol	0mg
Sodium	94mg
Total Carb.	36g
Dietary Fiber	1g
Protein	2g

Scalloped Carrots

Makes 10 servings

4 cups sliced carrots
3 tablespoons margarine
1 medium onion, chopped
1 10.75-ounce can cream of mushroom soup

1/2 teaspoon salt
1/2 cup grated cheddar cheese
3 cups seasoned bread crumbs
1/4 cup margarine, melted

In a large saucepan over medium-high heat, cook carrots with enough water to boil until tender. Drain.

In a large skillet, cook onion in 3 tablespoons of margarine until tender. Stir in soup, salt, cheese, and carrots. Pour into a greased 2-quart casserole.

In a small bowl, toss seasoned bread crumbs with 1/4 cup melted margarine (to cut down on fat, replace margarine with 1/4 cup hot water). Sprinkle over carrots. Bake in 350° F oven until heated through (about 30 minutes). Serve.

PER SERVING

Calories	176
Total Fat	14g
Sat. Fat	4g
Cholesterol	13mg
Sodium	420mg
Total Carb.	8g
Dietary Fiber	2g
Protein	4g

Squash Casserole

SARA TAYLOR (ADAPTED BY AUTHOR)

FriChik®

Makes 15 servings

2 pounds zucchini (or winter squash), sliced
1/4 cup chopped onion
1 10.75-ounce can cream of mushroom soup
1 cup fat-free sour cream
1 teaspoon McKay's® Chicken-style Seasoning

1 cup grated carrots
1 12 1/2-ounce can Worthington FriChik® (optional)
  (not included in with nutritional analysis)
1 8-ounce can seasoned dry bread crumbs
1/2 cup hot water

In a large kettle over medium-high heat, cook squash and onions in boiling, salted water for 5 minutes, drain.

In a large bowl, combine cream of mushroom soup, sour cream, and McKay's Chicken-style Seasoning. Stir in carrots, fold in drained squash, onions, and FriChik (if you choose to use it.) Mix well.

In a medium bowl, combine bread crumbs and boiling water. Spread half the bread crumb mixture in the bottom of a 9" x 13" baking dish. Spoon vegetable mixture on top. Sprinkle remaining bread crumbs over vegetable mixture. Bake at 350° F, covered, for 45 minutes.

PER SERVING

Calories	131
Total Fat	5g
Sat. Fat	3g
Cholesterol	0.5mg
Sodium	616mg
Total Carb.	16g
Dietary Fiber	2g
Protein	4g

Swiss-style Green Beans

Makes 8 servings

2 tablespoons margarine
1 tablespoon grated onion
1 8-ounce can sliced mushrooms, drained
1/2 teaspoon salt
1/2 cup finely-chopped green pepper
2 tablespoons flour

2 teaspoons granulated sugar
1 cup sour cream
1 cup grated Swiss cheese
2 pounds fresh green beans, ends trimmed,
  cooked and drained

In a large skillet over medium heat, saute onion, mushrooms, and green pepper in margarine till tender. Stir in flour, salt, and sugar to make a paste. Stir in sour cream until well blended. Remove from heat and stir in green beans and cheese. Turn into a greased 8" square baking dish. Top with 1 cup crushed corn flakes if desired. Bake at 350° F for 20 minutes or until bubbly.

PER SERVING

Calories	205
Total Fat	13g
Sat. Fat	7g
Cholesterol	28mg
Sodium	356mg
Total Carb.	14g
Dietary Fiber	5g
Protein	8g

Desserts

Caramel-Chocolate Chip Brownies

RUTH CRUMLEY

Makes 20 brownies

1 package German chocolate cake mix
3/4 cup margarine
1/3 cup evaporated milk
1 cup chopped walnuts
1 cup semisweet chocolate chips

Caramel mixture:
1/3 cup evaporated milk
12 ounces Kraft® caramels, unwrapped

With electric mixer, beat cake mix, margarine, and 1/3 cup milk for 2 minutes. Stir in walnuts by hand. Spoon 1/2 of the cake mixture into greased 9" x 13" pan. Spread mixture evenly. (For easier spreading place pan in preheated oven for one minute.) Bake at 350° F for 6 minutes. Remove from oven and sprinkle chocolate chips over the cake.

Melt Kraft caramels and milk in microwave or over low heat on top of stove. Drizzle over the chocolate chips. Drop remaining cake mixture over caramel sauce by teaspoons, as if making cookies *This will ease the spreading*. Bake another 15 minutes or until toothpick inserted in middle of brownies comes out clean. Allow to cool before cutting.

PER SERVING

Calories	338
Total Fat	18g
Sat. Fat	5g
Cholesterol	2mg
Sodium	306mg
Total Carb.	43g
Dietary Fiber	1g
Protein	4g

Chocolate Chip Bars

Makes 40 bars

1 cup shortening
3/4 cup granulated sugar
3/4 cup brown sugar, packed
2 medium eggs
1 tablespoon vanilla extract

2 1/4 cups unbleached white flour
1 teaspoon salt
1 teaspoon baking soda
1 12-ounce package semisweet chocolate chips

With electric mixer, cream shortening, sugars, eggs, and vanilla till creamy. Add flour, salt, and soda and beat well. Stir in chocolate chips. Evenly distribute into a greased 9" x 13" baking dish. Bake at 350° F for 20 to 25 minutes, or until golden brown. Cut into 40 pieces.

PER SERVING

Calories	140
Total Fat	8g
Sat. Fat	3g
Cholesterol	12mg
Sodium	183mg
Total Carb.	17g
Dietary Fiber	1g
Protein	1g

Magic Bars

Makes 20 bars

1/2 cup margarine
1 1/2 cups crushed graham crackers
1 14-ounce can sweetened condensed milk (not evaporated milk)
1 cup (6 ounces) semisweet chocolate chips
1 1/3 cups grated coconut
1 cup chopped walnuts

Preheat oven to 350° F.

In a 9" x 13" pan, melt margarine in oven. Sprinkle crushed graham crackers over margarine; mix together and press into pan. Pour sweetened condensed milk evenly over crumbs. Top evenly with chocolate chips, coconut, and chopped nuts. Bake for 25 to 30 minutes or until lightly browned. Cool before cutting.

PER SERVING

Calories	241
Total Fat	15g
Sat. Fat	6g
Cholesterol	7mg
Sodium	81mg
Total Carb.	25g
Dietary Fiber	1g
Protein	4g

Scotch-A-Roo Bars

Makes 25 bars

6 cups Rice Krispies® cereal
1 cup granulated sugar
1 cup light corn syrup
1 cup peanut butter (creamy or chunky)
1 cup semisweet chocolate chips
1 cup butterscotch chips

In a large bowl, measure Rice Krispies. Set aside.

In a medium saucepan over medium-high heat, combine sugar and corn syrup. Bring to a boil. Boil for exactly one minute. Remove from heat and add peanut butter. Stir until well blended. Pour over Rice Krispies and stir until cereal is well coated. Spread evenly into 9" x 13" greased cake pan.

Measure chocolate chips and butterscotch chips into a small glass bowl. Put in microwave for 1 to 1 1/2 minutes on high. Remove and stir well. Spread over Rice Krispies mixture. Cut into 25 pieces.

A hit with the kids—even older ones!

PER SERVING	
Calories	184
Total Fat	7g
Sat. Fat	2g
Cholesterol	0mg
Sodium	106mg
Total Carb.	29g
Dietary Fiber	1g
Protein	3g

Lemon Bars

MARIE SPANGLER

Makes 20 bars

2 cups unbleached white flour
1/2 cup powdered sugar
1 cup butter, softened (butter is best for this recipe)
4 eggs (or 1 cup egg substitute)

2 cups granulated sugar
1/4 cup plus 3 tablespoons lemon juice concentrate
1 tablespoon flour
1 cup chopped pecans

In a medium bowl, combine 2 cups flour and powdered sugar. Melt butter in microwave. Add butter to flour and sugar and mix well. Press into a 9" x 13" cake pan. Bake at 325° F for 15 minutes.

In a medium bowl, mix together eggs, sugar, lemon juice, flour, and pecans. Pour on top of crust. Bake at 325° F for 45 minutes. Remove from oven and sprinkle with powdered sugar while warm. Cut into squares.

PER SERVING

Calories	270
Total Fat	14g
Sat. Fat	6g
Cholesterol	67mg
Sodium	270mg
Total Carb.	33g
Dietary Fiber	1g
Protein	3g

Apple Burritos

Makes approximately 8 burritos

1 20-ounce can apple pie filling
8 flour tortillas

Lay tortilla on counter. Spoon 1/4 cup of apple filling into center of tortilla. Fold tortilla into a burrito. Place in casserole pan. To serve, heat in microwave. Garnish with a dollop of plain yogurt or fat-free sour cream.

A person completely wrapped up in himself makes a small package.

PER SERVING

Calories	162
Total Fat	2g
Sat. Fat	0.3g
Cholesterol	0mg
Sodium	168mg
Total Carb.	35g
Dietary Fiber	2g
Protein	2g

Chocolate-Caramel Extravaganza Cake

SUE LAZICH

Makes 15 servings

1 package Duncan Hines® Chocolate Cake Mix
3 eggs (or 3/4 cup egg substitute)
1 cup water
1/2 cup applesauce*

1 14-ounce can sweetened condensed milk
(not evaporated milk)
1 12-ounce jar caramel ice cream topping
1 8-ounce container Cool Whip®, thawed

Prepare cake mix with eggs, water, and applesauce according to package instructions. Pour batter into 9" x 13" cake pan. Bake at 350° F following package instructions. While cake is still warm, poke holes with the handle of a wooden spoon. Pour sweetened condensed milk over cake and into holes. Do the same with the caramel ice cream topping. When cool, cover cake with Cool Whip.

Yum. You can't stop with one piece but you should!

PER SERVING

Calories	330
Total Fat	9g
Sat. Fat	6g
Cholesterol	46mg
Sodium	427mg
Total Carb.	59g
Dietary Fiber	2g
Protein	5g

*replacement for oil

Sweethearts Dream Cake

CONNIE HATHAWAY

Makes 15 servings

1 package Duncan Hines® Yellow Cake Mix

3 eggs (or 3/4 cup egg substitute)

1 cup water

1/3 cup applesauce*

1 20-ounce can pineapple, undrained

3/4 cup granulated sugar

1 5.1-ounce package instant vanilla pudding mix

3 cups 1% low-fat milk

1 8-ounce container Cool Whip®, thawed

With electric mixer mix cake mix, eggs, water, and applesauce according to package. Bake in a 9" x 13" baking dish according to package. Remove from oven and poke holes in cake with the handle of a wooden spoon.

While cake is baking, in medium saucepan over medium-high heat, cook crushed pineapple, undrained and sugar for 20 minutes. Pour pineapple mixture over warm cake. Let cool.

Whip vanilla instant pudding and milk together until thickened. Spread over cake and pineapple topping. Refrigerate until set. Spread Cool Whip over pudding. Sprinkle toasted coconut on cake if desired. Refrigerate. Let sit Friday night. *Will be ready in time for potluck!*

*replacement for oil

PER SERVING	
Calories	297
Total Fat	8g
Sat. Fat	4g
Cholesterol	39mg
Sodium	358mg
Total Carb.	52g
Dietary Fiber	1g
Protein	4g

Chocolate Torte

GLENDA COURON

Makes 15 servings

1 cup unbleached white flour
1/2 cup margarine, melted
1/2 cup slivered almonds
1 cup powdered sugar

1 8-ounce package cream cheese, softened
1 16-ounce container Cool Whip®, thawed
3 3.4-ounce packages instant fudge pudding mix
5 cups 1% low-fat milk

Preheat oven to 350° F.

In a small bowl, mix flour, melted margarine, and slivered almonds. Press into a 9" x 13" cake pan. Bake 12 to 18 minutes or until golden brown. Remove from oven and cool.

In a medium bowl, combine powdered sugar and cream cheese. Mix either by hand or electric mixer. Gently fold in half the Cool Whip. Pour over cooled first layer and spread evenly.

In a large mixing bowl, combine pudding and milk. Using wire whisk, beat until it thickens. Place in refrigerator until it is set, 10 to 15 minutes, then pour over first two layers.

Spread the other half of the Cool Whip over the third layer. Refrigerate until ready to serve.

This is calorie-laden, but share those calories with others.

PER SERVING

Calories	342
Total Fat	16g
Sat. Fat	8g
Cholesterol	8mg
Sodium	519mg
Total Carb.	43g
Dietary Fiber	1g
Protein	5g

Apple Delight

ISABELLE EDMINSTER

Makes 15 servings

1 package yellow cake mix
1/2 cup margarine
1 20-ounce can apple (or cherry) pie filling
1 cup sour cream
1 egg

In a large bowl, prepare the dry cake mix and margarine as you would a pie crust. Pat into ungreased pizza pan or 9" x 13" cake pan. Pour prepared apple (or cherry) filling over crust. In a small bowl, beat sour cream and egg. Drizzle over the apples. Bake at 350° F for 25 minutes or until sour cream is golden brown. Slice into 15 pieces.

PER SERVING	
Calories	269
Total Fat	13g
Sat. Fat	4g
Cholesterol	19mg
Sodium	336mg
Total Carb.	36g
Dietary Fiber	0.6g
Protein	2g

Dump Cake

ALICE WILLSEY

Makes 15 servings

1 20-ounce can crushed pineapple, undrained
1 20-ounce can cherry pie filling
1 package yellow cake mix
2 cups chopped walnuts
1/2 cup margarine

Dump crushed pineapple and cherry pie filling into a 9" x 13" cake pan. Pour dry cake mix over fruit. Cover with walnuts (or pecans). Melt margarine and pour evenly over walnuts. Bake at 350° F for 55 minutes. Cool.

PER SERVING

Calories	363
Total Fat	19g
Sat. Fat	2g
Cholesterol	1mg
Sodium	304mg
Total Carb.	44g
Dietary Fiber	2g
Protein	6g

Fresh Apple Cake With Crumb Topping

Makes 15 servings

1 cup granulated sugar
1/3 cup shortening
1 1/2 cups unbleached white flour
1 teaspoon baking soda
1/2 teaspoon salt
1 egg
2 cups grated apples

1 teaspoon vanilla extract
1 teaspoon ground cinnamon

Topping:
1/2 cup brown sugar
2 tablespoons unbleached white flour
3 tablespoons margarine

With electric mixer, cream sugar and shortening. Add other ingredients and beat until well mixed. Pour into greased 9" x 13" cake pan.

In a small bowl, combine brown sugar, flour, and margarine and mix until coarse. Sprinkle over cake batter. Bake at 375° F for 35 to 45 minutes, or until a toothpick inserted into center of cake comes out clean. No frosting is necessary. If desired, serve warm with Cool Whip or whipped cream.

PER SERVING	
Calories	193
Total Fat	7g
Sat. Fat	2g
Cholesterol	15mg
Sodium	366mg
Total Carb.	30g
Dietary Fiber	1g
Protein	2g

Lemon Jell-☆ Cake

PAUL RICCHIUTI

Makes 15 servings

1 package lemon or yellow cake mix
1 6-ounce package lemon Jell-O®
3/4 cup canola oil
3/4 cup hot water

4 eggs

Sauce:
1/2 cup lemon juice concentrate
1 1/2 cups powdered sugar

With electric mixer, beat cake mix, Jell-O, oil, hot water, and eggs according to cake package instructions. Pour into greased 9" x 13" cake pan. Bake at 350° F for 35 minutes or until toothpick inserted into center of cake comes out clean. While cake is hot, punch holes all over the top with the handle of a wooden spoon.

In a small bowl, combine lemon juice and powdered sugar. Pour into holes made by wooden spoon. Refrigerate until ready to serve. *It is not necessary to frost this cake, because it is so moist by itself, but you may chose to top with fat-free Cool Whip.*

PER SERVING

Calories	331
Total Fat	15g
Sat. Fat	2g
Cholesterol	50mg
Sodium	271mg
Total Carb.	45g
Dietary Fiber	0.3g
Protein	3g

Mystery Cake With Crumb Topping

Makes 15 servings

1 1/2 cups unbleached white flour
1 cup granulated sugar
1 egg (or 1/4 cup egg substitute)
1 teaspoon baking soda
Pinch of salt

1 16-ounce can fruit cocktail, undrained
Topping:
1 cup brown sugar
1/2 cup chopped walnuts

In a large bowl, combine all ingredients—except fruit cocktail. Add undrained fruit cocktail and gently stir from the bottom. Pour into greased 9" x 13" cake pan.

In a small bowl, combine brown sugar and walnuts; sprinkle over cake mixture. Bake at 350° F for 45 to 60 minutes, or until a toothpick inserted into middle of cake comes out clean. Serve warm or cold.

Yummy!

PER SERVING	
Calories	162
Total Fat	3g
Sat. Fat	0.3g
Cholesterol	12mg
Sodium	250mg
Total Carb.	32g
Dietary Fiber	1g
Protein	3g

Raspberry Poke Cake

Makes 15 servings

1 package white cake mix
1 1/3 cup water
2 eggs (or 1/2 cup egg substitute)
1/3 cup applesauce*

1 3-ounce package raspberry Jell-O®
1 cup boiling water
1/2 cup cold water
1 8-ounce container Cool Whip®, thawed

Prepare cake mix as package directs using water, eggs, and applesauce. Pour mixture into greased 9" x 13" cake pan. Bake at 350° F for 30 minutes or until toothpick inserted into center of cake comes out clean. Cool. Using a large fork, poke the cake at 1/2" intervals.

In a medium bowl, dissolve gelatin in boiling water. Add cold water. Slowly pour gelatin over cake, filling holes left by fork. Chill in refrigerator until gelatin is set. Frost with Cool Whip. Keep refrigerated till ready to serve.

This is a very refreshing dessert.

PER SERVING

Calories	222
Total Fat	7g
Sat. Fat	4g
Cholesterol	25mg
Sodium	254mg
Total Carb.	34g
Dietary Fiber	0g
Protein	3g

*replacement for oil

Strawberry Yogurt Cake

KAREN MCFADDEN

Makes 15 servings

1 package strawberry (or white) cake mix
3/4 cup cold water
3/4 cup (6 ounces) strawberry yogurt
1/3 cup canola oil

3 eggs (or 3/4 cup egg substitute)
Frosting:
4 cups thawed Cool Whip®
3/4 cup (6 ounces) strawberry yogurt

Prepare cake mix according to package using water, 3/4 cup strawberry yogurt, oil, and eggs. Beat for 3 minutes. Pour into greased 9" x 13" cake pan or two 9" round cake pans that have been greased and floured well. Bake at 350° F according to package instructions. Cool. (If using round pans, invert pans onto wire rack to cool.)

In a large bowl, gently fold 3/4 cup yogurt into Cool Whip, mixing well. Spread evenly on 9" x 13" cake. For round cake, place first layer on a platter. Use some of the frosting for the filling. Place other round layer on top of filling. Spread remainder of frosting on sides and top.

SERVING SUGGESTION: This cake looks beautiful when garnished with whole fresh strawberries (including stems).

PER SERVING

Calories	311
Total Fat	15g
Sat. Fat	7g
Cholesterol	39mg
Sodium	256mg
Total Carb.	40g
Dietary Fiber	0g
Protein	3g

Easy Carrot Cake

SUE SHABO

Makes 15 servings

1 cup canola oil
2 cups granulated sugar
3 eggs
2 cups grated carrots
1 20-ounce can crushed pineapple, undrained

2 teaspoons ground cinnamon
2 teaspoons baking soda
1 teaspoon salt
1 cup grated coconut
2 cups unbleached white flour

In a large bowl, combine ingredients and stir until mixed. *Easy, huh!* Pour into greased 9" x 13" cake pan and bake at 350° F for 45 minutes or until a toothpick inserted into center of cake comes out clean. Cool.

SERVING SUGGESTION: This can be served with or without cream cheese frosting.

Cream Cheese Frosting:

1 3-ounce package cream cheese, softened
1 tablespoon milk
1 teaspoon vanilla

Dash salt
2 1/2 cups powdered sugar

In a small bowl, blend cream cheese, milk, vanilla, and salt. Gradually add sugar, beating until frosting is smooth.

PER SERVING

Calories	330
Total Fat	17g
Sat. Fat	3g
Cholesterol	37mg
Sodium	552mg
Total Carb.	42g
Dietary Fiber	1g
Protein	3g

Pistachio Pudding Cake

Makes 15 servings

1/3 cup chopped pecans
1/3 cup granulated sugar
2 tablespoons ground cinnamon
1 package white cake mix
1 3.4-ounce package instant pistachio pudding

4 eggs (or 1 cup egg substitute)
1 cup sour cream
3/4 cup orange juice
2 tablespoons canola oil
1 teaspoon vanilla extract

Spray a bundt pan with non-stick cooking spray.

In a small bowl, combine pecans, sugar, and cinnamon. Sprinkle 1/3 of pecan mixture into bundt pan bottom and sides.

With electric mixer, combine cake mix and remaining ingredients. Beat until thickened.

Alternate layers of batter with remaining nut mixture into bundt pan. Swirl with a fork. Bake at 350° F for 35 to 45 minutes or until a toothpick inserted into cake comes out clean.

PER SERVING

Calories	279
Total Fat	12g
Sat. Fat	3g
Cholesterol	56mg
Sodium	337mg
Total Carb.	40g
Dietary Fiber	1g
Protein	4g

Oatmeal Cake With Coconut Frosting

RUTH COLVIN

Makes 15 servings

1 1/4 cups boiling water
1 cup old-fashioned rolled oats
1 cup brown sugar
1 cup granulated sugar
1 1/3 cups unbleached white flour
1/2 teaspoon salt
1 teaspoon ground cinnamon
1 teaspoon ground nutmeg
1 teaspoon baking soda
2 eggs (or 1/2 cup egg substitute)
1/2 cup margarine

Coconut frosting:

6 tablespoons margarine
1 cup chopped walnuts
1/2 cup brown sugar
1/4 cup evaporated skim milk
1/2 teaspoon vanilla extract
1 cup grated coconut

PER SERVING	
Calories	363
Total Fat	18g
Sat. Fat	4g
Cholesterol	25mg
Sodium	447mg
Total Carb.	45g
Dietary Fiber	2g
Protein	6g

In a large bowl, pour boiling water over oatmeal. Let stand 20 minutes. Add other cake ingredients and mix well. Pour into greased 9" x 13" cake pan. Bake cake at 350° F for 45 minutes or until toothpick inserted into center of cake comes out clean.

In a small saucepan over medium heat, melt 6 tablespoons margarine. Add other frosting ingredients and warm until sugar dissolves. Remove from heat. Spread over cake while still warm. Serve warm. *This can be reheated in oven or microwave before serving for potluck.*

Old Fashioned Gingerbread Cake

Makes 15 servings

2 1/2 cups unbleached white flour
1 1/2 teaspoons baking soda
1 teaspoon ground ginger
3/4 teaspoon ground cinnamon
1/4 teaspoon ground cloves
1/4 teaspoon salt

1/2 cup shortening*
1/2 cup granulated sugar
1 cup molasses
1 egg (or 1/4 cup egg substitute)
1 cup cold water

In a large bowl, combine all dry ingredients. Set aside.

In a medium bowl, combine shortening, molasses, egg, and water. Pour all at once into dry ingredients. Mix together either by hand or electric mixer until thoroughly combined. Pour into greased 9" x 12" cake pan. Bake at 350° F for 30 minutes or until a toothpick inserted into center of cake comes out clean. Serve warm with a whipped topping.

*1/4 cup Prune Whip can be substituted (see p. 155). This dessert will then be fat-free.

PER SERVING	
Calories	224
Total Fat	7g
Sat. Fat	3g
Cholesterol	16mg
Sodium	441mg
Total Carb.	37g
Dietary Fiber	1g
Protein	2g

Cheesecake With Granola Crust

GLENDA COURON

Makes 15 servings

3 cups granola
1/3 cup margarine, melted
2 tablespoons evaporated milk
2 8-ounce packages cream cheese, softened
1 cup granulated sugar

2 tablespoons lemon juice concentrate
1/4 cup milk
1 16-ounce container Cool Whip®, thawed
1 20-ounce can cherry pie filling

In blender, grind granola till fine. Pour granola into large bowl. Add melted margarine and evaporated milk. Mix well and press into 9" x 13" cake pan. Set aside.

In a large bowl, beat softened cream cheese with electric mixer. Add sugar, lemon juice, and milk. Beat until smooth. Gently fold in Cool Whip until mixed. Spread cream cheese mixture over granola crust. Refrigerate. Spread cherry pie filling evenly over cream cheese mixture.

PER SERVING

Calories	364
Total Fat	20g
Sat. Fat	10g
Cholesterol	14mg
Sodium	94mg
Total Carb.	43g
Dietary Fiber	3g
Protein	5g

Swiss Cherry Cheese Torte

Makes 16 servings

1 package Swiss chocolate cake mix
3 eggs (or 3/4 cup egg substitute)
1 1/3 cups water
1/3 cup applesauce*

4 ounces cream cheese, softened
2 teaspoons lemon juice concentrate
1 container prepared vanilla frosting
1 20-ounce can cherry pie filling

Prepare cake mix according to instructions using eggs, water, and applesauce. Pour into two greased and floured round cake pans. Bake according to instructions on box. Cool on wire racks. Split each layer when cooled.

Cream together cream cheese and lemon juice until smooth. Fold in vanilla frosting. Spread frosting mixture first then pie filling between layers and on top of cake. Refrigerate until ready to serve.

*substitute for oil

PER SERVING	
Calories	344
Total Fat	11g
Sat. Fat	3g
Cholesterol	8mg
Sodium	313mg
Total Carb.	59g
Dietary Fiber	1g
Protein	2g

Debby's Easy Cream Cheese Cherry Pie

Makes 8 servings

1 prepared graham cracker crust
1 8-ounce package cream cheese, softened
1 14-ounce can sweetened condensed milk (not evaporated milk)
1/3 cup lemon juice concentrate
1 teaspoon vanilla extract
1 20-ounce can cherry pie filling

In a medium bowl, beat softened cream cheese until fluffy. Gradually add sweetened condensed milk and mix on low speed, scraping sides until well blended. Add lemon juice and vanilla and mix till blended. Pour into prepared crust. Pour cherry pie filling over cream cheese mixture. Refrigerate until ready to serve.

Super easy and a big hit with men! They will think you cooked all day.

PER SERVING

Calories	396
Total Fat	14g
Sat. Fat	6g
Cholesterol	24mg
Sodium	259mg
Total Carb.	63g
Dietary Fiber	1g
Protein	5g

Quick Strawberry Pie

Makes 10 servings

1/2 cup margarine
1 cup unbleached white flour
3 tablespoons powdered sugar
2 to 3 pints fresh strawberries

1 cup cold water
1 cup granulated sugar
3 tablespoons cornstarch
3 tablespoons strawberry Jell-O®

In a medium bowl, cut margarine into flour and powdered sugar—pie crust style. Pat into 9" pie plate. Bake for 20 to 25 minutes at 325° F. Cool. Heap fresh strawberries—pyramid style—into pie crust.

In a medium saucepan over medium-high heat, combine water, sugar, cornstarch, and strawberry Jell-O. Cook until thickened. Cool. Pour over strawberries. Refrigerate until ready to serve.

PER SERVING

Calories	259
Total Fat	10g
Sat. Fat	1g
Cholesterol	0mg
Sodium	163mg
Total Carb.	421g
Dietary Fiber	3g
Protein	2g

Apple Brown Betty

Makes 15 servings

6 cups sliced apples
2 cups old-fashioned rolled oats
1 cup chopped walnuts
1 cup whole wheat flour
2 teaspoons ground cinnamon
1/2 teaspoon ground nutmeg

1/2 teaspoon salt
1/2 cup canola oil
1/2 cup honey
2 teaspoons vanilla
1 teaspoon lemon extract

Slice peeled and cored cooking apples into a 9" x 13" baking dish.

In a medium bowl, mix remaining ingredients till crumbly. Cover apples with topping. Bake at 350° F until apples are tender and topping is golden brown (35 to 45 minutes). Serve warm with a scoop of ice cream.

PER SERVING

Calories	283
Total Fat	13g
Sat. Fat	1g
Cholesterol	0mg
Sodium	79mg
Total Carb.	36g
Dietary Fiber	4g
Protein	7g

Apple-Cranberry Crisp

Makes 9 servings

1 16-ounce can whole cranberry sauce
2 tablespoons cornstarch
5 cups peeled, cored, and thinly-sliced
  Granny Smith apples

Topping:
1 1/2 cups old-fashioned oatmeal
1/2 cup brown sugar
1/3 cup unbleached white flour
1/2 teaspoon ground cinnamon
1/3 cup margarine, melted
1 tablespoon water

In a large saucepan, combine cranberry sauce and cornstarch. Heat and stir occasionally until bubbly. Add apples and cook for 2 more minutes. Spoon apples into 8" square baking dish.

In a medium bowl, mix remaining ingredients. Crumble over apples. Bake at 350° F for 30 to 35 minutes, or until bubbly. Serve warm or cold.

PER SERVING	
Calories	325
Total Fat	9g
Sat. Fat	1g
Cholesterol	0mg
Sodium	77mg
Total Carb.	59g
Dietary Fiber	4g
Protein	5g

Candy Land Dessert

LuWana Kumalae

Makes 20 servings

2 3/4-ounce packages instant vanilla pudding mix
1 quart vanilla ice cream, softened
2 cups 1% low-fat milk
1 pound butter cookies, crushed

1/2 cup butter, melted
1 8-ounce container Cool Whip®, thawed
3 Skor candy bars, finely chopped (optional)

In a large bowl, mix vanilla pudding, softened ice cream, and milk. Set aside.

In a large bowl, mix crushed butter cookies and melted butter. Spread evenly into a 9" x 13" cake pan. Bake at 350° F for 15 minutes. Cool. Spread filling on top of cooled crust. Refrigerate overnight. Before serving, spread Cool Whip over dessert and, if desired, sprinkle finely-chopped Skor bars over Cool Whip. Always keep refrigerated.

PER SERVING

Calories	272
Total Fat	14g
Sat. Fat	9g
Cholesterol	45mg
Sodium	282mg
Total Carb.	33g
Dietary Fiber	0g
Protein	3g

Mud Pie

MARY HAMES

Makes 10 servings

1 1/4 cups chocolate cookie crumbs
1/4 cup granulated sugar
1/4 cup margarine, melted
1/2 gallon [your favorite] ice cream, softened
1 12-ounce jar chocolate fudge ice-cream topping

In a medium bowl, mix cookie crumbs, sugar, and melted margarine. Press into 9" springform pan and chill in freezer. Slightly soften a half-gallon of your favorite ice cream. (Mocha Almond Fudge or Cookies and Cream are wonderful in this dessert.) Remove springform pan from freezer and spread ice cream evenly over crust. Place back in freezer and let set till hard.

When it's time to set up the dessert table at potluck, remove the Mud Pie from the freezer and top with chocolate fudge ice-cream topping. Use the whole jar and spread evenly over ice cream. Take the sides off of the springform pan and slice into 10 pieces. Garnish with whipped cream and slivered almonds, if desired.

This is easy to make. A real favorite—just remember to put it in the freezer when you get to church.

There is no happiness in having or in getting, but only in giving.

PER SERVING

Calories	472
Total Fat	21g
Sat. Fat	9g
Cholesterol	36mg
Sodium	279mg
Total Carb.	66g
Dietary Fiber	2g
Protein	5g

Old-Fashioned Bread Pudding

Makes 20 servings

1 pound French bread
4 cups skim milk
2 cups granulated sugar
3 eggs (or 3/4 cup egg substitute)
1 1/4 cups raisins
1 cup chopped pecans (optional)
2 tablespoons vanilla extract

Imitation rum sauce:

1/4 cup sugar
1 tablespoon cornstarch
1 cup skim milk
1/8 teaspoon salt
1 1/2 teaspoons imitation rum extract
1 teaspoon margarine
1 teaspoon vanilla extract

Tear or cut bread into 1" pieces. Place in a large bowl. Add milk and let stand until milk is absorbed into bread.

In a large bowl, combine sugar eggs, raisins, nuts, and vanilla. Beat till mixed. Add to bread mixture, stirring well. Pour into greased 9" x 13" pan. Bake at 350° F for 40 minutes or until set.

In a small saucepan over medium-high heat, mix sugar, cornstarch, milk, and salt. Bring to a boil and cook until thickened. Remove from heat and add rum extract, margarine, and vanilla.

Serve pudding warm with warm rum sauce.

Delicious.

PER SERVING

Calories	205
Total Fat	1g
Sat. Fat	0.5g
Cholesterol	29mg
Sodium	194mg
Total Carb.	42g
Dietary Fiber	1g
Protein	5g

Wheat Berry Dessert

Makes 12 servings

1 1/2 cups uncooked wheat berries
4 cups thawed Cool Whip® (or 1 8-ounce container)
1 8-ounce package cream cheese, softened
2 cups sour cream
2 3.4-ounce packages instant vanilla (or lemon) pudding mix
1 20-ounce can pineapple chunks, undrained

In a medium pan, cook wheat berries over medium heat until tender but chewy, keeping covered with water at all times. Drain and cool.

In a large bowl, combine remaining ingredients, adding wheat berries last. Refrigerate in large serving bowl until ready to serve. Garnish with strawberries, if desired.

Swallow your pride occasionally. It's not fattening.

PER SERVING

Calories	330
Total Fat	20g
Sat. Fat	13g
Cholesterol	38mg
Sodium	315mg
Total Carb.	33g
Dietary Fiber	2g
Protein	7g

SECTION 7

Miscellaneous

Alfredo Sauce

Yields 2 cups (approximately 6 servings)

1/4 cup margarine
2 tablespoons dried sweet basil
2 tablespoons dried parsley
1 8-ounce package cream cheese, softened

1/4 cup olive oil
1/3 cup grated Parmesan cheese
2 cloves garlic, minced

In a medium saucepan, melt margarine. Add herbs. Add cream cheese, stirring occasionally until melted. Add olive oil, garlic, and Parmesan and blend well. Remove from heat before sauce comes to a boil. Serve hot.

HEALTHY CHOICE

2 tablespoons margarine
2 tablespoons flour
1/4 teaspoon salt
1 cup skim milk

2 tablespoons dried sweet basil
2 tablespoons dried parsley
1 8-ounce package fat-free cream cheese, softened
2 cloves garlic, minced

In a medium saucepan, melt margarine. Add flour and salt and stir. Add milk and stir mixture until thickened. Add fat-free cream cheese, herbs, and garlic. Stir until cream cheese melts. Serve hot.

SERVING SUGGESTION: Serve over any kind of pasta. Especially good on angel hair and linguine.

Life isn't fair, but God is!

PER SERVING	
Calories	309
Total Fat	31g
Sat. Fat	12g
Cholesterol	46mg
Sodium	217mg
Total Carb.	2g
Dietary Fiber	0.5g
Protein	6g

LITE SERVING	
Calories	60
Total Fat	1g
Sat. Fat	0g
Cholesterol	6mg
Sodium	255mg
Total Carb.	6g
Dietary Fiber	0g
Protein	6g

Divan Cream Sauce

2 1/4 cups (approximately 15 servings)

2 tablespoons margarine
2 tablespoons flour
1 cup skim milk
1 tablespoon lemon juice concentrate
1 cup sour cream

In a medium saucepan over medium heat, melt margarine. Add flour to make a thick paste. Slowly add milk and whisk till smooth. Cook until thickened. Remove from heat and add lemon juice and sour cream and whisk until smooth. Serve warm.

SERVING SUGGESTION: Spoon over patties or roasts. Can be used on vegetables as well.

PER SERVING

Calories	56
Total Fat	5g
Sat. Fat	2g
Cholesterol	7mg
Sodium	30mg
Total Carb.	2g
Dietary Fiber	0g
Protein	42g

Pimiento "Cheese" Sauce I

Yields 2 1/2 cups (approximately 12 servings)

1 cup cold water
1 cup cashews
2 tablespoons sesame seeds
1 1/4 teaspoons salt
1/4 cup brewer's yeast flakes

1/4 cup canola oil
1 teaspoon onion powder
Dash of salt
1/2 cup canned pimientos, drained
1/3 cup lemon juice concentrate

In blender on high blend water, nuts, sesame seeds, salt, and brewer's yeast. Slowly, through blender lid, add oil, onion powder, salt, pimientos, and lemon juice. Blend until smooth.

SERVING SUGGESTION: This is a tasty substitute for cheese. Use in lasagna or for vegetables.

PER SERVING

Calories	165
Total Fat	12g
Sat. Fat	2g
Cholesterol	0mg
Sodium	289mg
Total Carb.	10g
Dietary Fiber	0.6g
Protein	10g

Pimiento "Cheese" Sauce II

ANN THRASH-TRUMBO

Yields 2 cups (approximately 12 servings)

1 cup cold water
3/4 cup leftover cooked breakfast cereal
  (such as oatmeal, millet, or barley)
1 1/4 teaspoons salt
3 tablespoons brewer's yeast flakes

2 teaspoons onion powder
1/4 teaspoon garlic powder
1/4 teaspoon dill seed
2 tablespoons tomato paste
2 tablespoons lemon juice concentrate

Put all ingredients in blender. Blend till very smooth—this may take 2 to 3 minutes at high speed. *Wear ear protection!*

SERVING SUGGESTION: This delicious sauce is useful for potluck favorites such as lasagna (mixed with tofu in place of mozzarella cheese). Use this as a substitute for cheese.

PER SERVING

Calories	63
Total Fat	1g
Sat. Fat	0.1
Cholesterol	0mg
Sodium	250mg
Total Carb.	8g
Dietary Fiber	1g
Protein	8g

Tomato Gravy

Yields 2 1/2 cups

1/4 cup margarine
2 tablespoons diced onion
1/4 cup unbleached white flour
2 cups tomato juice
1 teaspoon celery salt
1 teaspoon salt

In a medium skillet, saute onion in margarine until tender. Blend in flour and seasonings. Slowly add tomato juice and mix with a wire whisk. Bring to a simmer. Simmer 5 minutes.

SERVING SUGGESTION: Great over roasts or patties.

Sensuous Sauce

Yields 1 1/2 quarts

1/4 cup canola oil
4 cloves garlic
1/4 cup unbleached white flour
1/4 cup chili powder

2 teaspoons ground cumin
1 46-fluid ounce can tomato juice
Salt to taste

In a large kettle over medium-high heat, saute garlic cloves (left whole) in oil for 2 minutes. Add flour, chili powder, and cumin. Saute for 1 minute to bring out flavors. Add tomato juice and stir until there are no lumps. Add salt to taste. Bring to boil, then remove from heat.

SERVING SUGGESTION: This sauce can be used over haystacks, as a tortilla chip dip, or served with hot dogs. The uses are limitless.

This sauce gets its name from the way it tantalizingly smells up the house.

Peanut Sauce

Yields 1 cup (approximately 6 servings)

1/2 cup peanut butter (creamy or chunky)
1/2 cup boiling water
2 tablespoons soy sauce
2 tablespoons lemon juice concentrate

1 teaspoon ground ginger
1 teaspoon sesame oil
1/2 teaspoon minced garlic

In a small bowl, combine ingredients. Whip with wire whisk until creamy.

SERVING SUGGESTION: Toss with your favorite pastas or use as a dressing for a pita sandwich.

PER SERVING	
Calories	140
Total Fat	12g
Sat. Fat	2g
Cholesterol	0mg
Sodium	444mg
Total Carb.	5g
Dietary Fiber	1g
Protein	6g

Sesame Sauce

Yields 2/3 cup

1/2 cup sesame seeds
3 tablespoons canola oil
Juice of one lemon

In a small skillet over medium-heat, heat oil. Add sesame seeds and stir until browned. Remove from heat, add lemon juice, and stir.

SERVING SUGGESTION: Serve over steamed broccoli or cauliflower.

Easy Sweet & Sour Sauce

Yields 1 cup

1 cup reduced-calorie apricot spread
1 tablespoon vinegar (or lemon juice)
1 tablespoon lemon juice concentrate
2 teaspoons soy sauce

In a medium glass bowl, combine ingredients. Microwave on high for 5 minutes.

SERVING SUGGESTION: This sauce can be used for any sweet and sour entree or vegetable.

☆Oriental Sweet and Sour Sauce

Yields 2 3/4 cups

1 1/2 cups unsweetened pineapple juice
1/2 cup + 2 tablespoons brown sugar
1/2 cup apple cider vinegar (or lemon juice concentrate)
1/4 teaspoon garlic powder
2 tablespoons cornstarch
1/4 cup soy sauce

In a large saucepan over medium-high heat, combine all ingredients. Whisk out all lumps and stir constantly until thickened.

AUTHOR'S NOTE: This is the sauce I use with my meatballs (see p. 47). Just pour over meatballs in a 9" x 13" pan. Heat until bubbly.

Yum! A real taste of the Orient.

Cucumber Cheese Spread

Yields 1 3/4 cup (24 servings)

1 8-ounce package fat-free cream cheese, softened
1/2 cup grated cucumber, drained
1/4 cup finely-chopped onion
1 tablespoon finely-chopped fresh parsley
1/4 teaspoon salt

In a large bowl, whip softened cream cheese with electric beater until fluffy. Stir in the cucumber, onion, parsley, and salt; mix well. Refrigerate.

SERVING SUGGESTION: This is a refreshing spread and is great with crackers, bread, or as a sandwich filling.

PER SERVING

Calories	11
Total Fat	0g
Sat. Fat	0g
Cholesterol	2mg
Sodium	71mg
Total Carb.	1g
Dietary Fiber	0g
Protein	1g

Soybean Spread

Yields 2 cups (approximately 16 servings)

2 tablespoons canola oil
1 small onion, finely chopped
1 clove garlic, minced
2 tablespoons finely-chopped fresh parsley

2 cups cooked, ground soybeans
1 teaspoon ground oregano
1 tablespoon soy sauce
1/3 cup fat-free Miracle Whip (or mayonnaise)

In a small skillet, saute onion and garlic in oil. Remove from heat and add parsley.

In a medium bowl, add ground soybeans, oregano, soy sauce, mayonnaise, and sauteed mixture. Mix well. Refrigerate until ready to serve. *This keeps well in the refrigerator.*

SERVING SUGGESTION: Use as a spread for crackers or sandwiches.

PER SERVING

Calories	57
Total Fat	3g
Sat. Fat	1g
Cholesterol	0mg
Sodium	107mg
Total Carb.	3g
Dietary Fiber	0.1g
Protein	4g

Creamy Carrot-Leek Dip

Yields 5 cups (approximately 40 servings)

1 package dehydrated leek soup mix
2 cups sour cream
1/2 cup fat-free Miracle Whip® (or mayonnaise)
1 tablespoon snipped fresh dill weed
2 cups grated carrots
1 cup chopped radishes

In a medium bowl, combine all ingredients. Store in refrigerator covered for at least 2 hours.

SERVING SUGGESTION: Arrange a vegetable platter and place a dish of this dip in the middle. Also good for replacing mayonnaise in sandwiches.

PER SERVING

Calories	38
Total Fat	3g
Sat. Fat	2g
Cholesterol	5mg
Sodium	134mg
Total Carb.	3g
Dietary Fiber	0g
Protein	1g

Spinach Dip

SANDI GOLLES

Yields 4 1/2 cups (approximately 40 servings)

1 10-ounce package frozen chopped spinach, thawed
2 cups sour cream
1 cup fat-free Miracle Whip® (or mayonnaise)
1/2 cup finely-chopped fresh parsley

1/2 cup chopped green onion
1 package dehydrated leek soup mix
1/2 teaspoon dried dill weed
1 teaspoon Italian seasoning

Squeeze spinach until dry.

In a large bowl, combine spinach and remainder of ingredients. Stir well. Refrigerate overnight.

SERVING SUGGESTION: Great as a dip with a vegetable platter or chips.

PER SERVING

Calories	40
Total Fat	3g
Sat. Fat	2g
Cholesterol	5mg
Sodium	163mg
Total Carb.	3g
Dietary Fiber	0g
Protein	1g

Strawberry-Marshmallow Fruit Dip

Yields 3 cups (approximately 32 servings)

1 7-ounce jar marshmallow creme
1 8-ounce tub Philadelphia® Brand strawberry-flavored cream cheese

In a medium bowl, stir together marshmallow cream and strawberry cream cheese. Chill till ready to serve.

SERVING SUGGESTION: Arrange a platter of fresh fruits, placing this dip in a small bowl in the center.

PER SERVING

Calories	30
Total Fat	1g
Sat. Fat	1g
Cholesterol	3mg
Sodium	2mg
Total Carb.	4g
Dietary Fiber	0g
Protein	0.2g

Pooh Butter

Yields 2 1/2 cups (approximately 40 servings)

For Kids

1 cup butter or margarine, softened
1 cup peanut butter (creamy or chunky)
1/4 cup honey

With electric mixer, whip softened butter until fluffy. Add peanut butter and beat till mixed, then add honey and whip until light and creamy.

SERVING SUGGESTION: Use it as a spread on bread. Keep unused portion in the refrigerator. Take out 1/2 hour before serving so it will be softened.

Yum! Kids, you will love this, and it is so easy to make.

PER SERVING

Calories	85
Total Fat	8g
Sat. Fat	1g
Cholesterol	0mg
Sodium	30mg
Total Carb.	3g
Dietary Fiber	0.4g
Protein	1.7g

Prune Whip

Yields 1 cup

OIL SUBSTITUTE FOR BAKING DESSERTS OR BREADS

1 1/3 cups pitted prunes
1/4 cup + 2 tablespoons hot water

In blender, combine pitted prunes and hot water. Blend on high speed, scraping down sides until smooth.

I learned the hard way that just because the package says "pitted prunes" does not mean there will not be a pit. Squeeze each prune before putting it in the blender.

MEASUREMENTS FOR SUBSTITUTIONS:

OIL OR BUTTER	PRUNE WHIP
1 cup	1/2 cup
3/4 cup	1/4 cup + 2 tablespoons
2/3 cup	1/3 cup
1/2 cup	1/4 cup
1/3 cup	2 tablespoons + 2 teaspoons
1/4 cup	2 tablespoons

Zapping the Fat and Cholesterol

There's a lot of concern these days, and rightly so, about the amount of fat that was included in some of our old favorite recipes. Many of those recipes had been handed down from mother to daughter for generations. They probably originated in a farm kitchen where workers who had spent the morning tossing hay bales needed lots of calories quick. After lunch they'd go back to work and burn off another thousand calories before the sun set.

That's not what most Adventists do after potluck!

Cholesterol is another important concern, and eggs, whole milk, and cheese add a lot of that to recipes. You can modify many recipes to eliminate these villains using the suggestions below:

CUTTING OUT THE CHOLESTEROL

Egg whites don't contain any cholesterol, so if you don't feel a need to cut out eggs altogether, remember that the whites of two large eggs make 1/4 cup of egg whites. I've noted that as an alternative in many recipes that call for eggs. Of course you can also purchase commercial egg substitutes such as Morningstar Farms Scramblers® or EggBeaters®, but that works out to be more expensive than just throwing out the yolks (or feeding them to your cat or dog—they're better equipped for handling the cholesterol) and using the whites.

In baking I have often used a product called Egg Replacer®, which is available in many food co-ops and health food stores. It uses potato starch and tapioca flour to add the bonding qualities of eggs to the recipe. It has zero fat and zero cholesterol and is very inexpensive compared to the cost of eggs.

When a recipe calls for milk, I've never experienced any problem when I simply used soy milk, rice milk, or skim milk in place of whole milk. Using any of these products will cut out the cholesterol. Be aware that some soy milk products are nearly as high in fat as whole milk, but they don't have as much saturated fat as regular milk.

To cut back on cheese, consider some of the commercial products at stores, including tofu cheese. I've included two recipes for "pimiento cheese sauce" in this book, and either of these will work well in recipes like lasagna and pizza. I've never tried them in a grilled cheese sandwich, though!

I've had good success using low-fat or no-fat sour cream and cream cheese in recipes as well. Sometimes there is a bit of change in texture or moistness noticeable, but you can often adjust for this by adding a bit of milk or milk substitute. Also, do be aware that some of these products are quite high in sodium.

CUTTING BACK ON FAT

To further cut back the fat calories in a baked recipe, check out the Prune Whip recipe on page 155. It works great in place of oil, and instructions for substitution are included with the recipe. Many people use applesauce in place of oil in cake recipes.

Mushroom soup is a popular ingredient in many potluck recipes. What most people don't realize is that the regular Campbell's® version gets nearly two-thirds of its calories from fat. Adding a can to your recipe really drives the fat and calorie count up fast. Fortunately Campbell's® has recently come out with a Healthy Request® version that has only six grams of fat instead of the 23 grams in the regular version. It seems to work just fine in recipes that call for mushroom soup, and it is much lower in sodium as well.

Index

Commercial Product Index